PATCHES OF SUNLIGHT,
OR OF SHADOW

THE SWISS LIST

Philippe Jaccottet

PATCHES OF SUNLIGHT, OR OF SHADOW

SAFEGUARDED NOTES
1952–2005

Translated by John Taylor

LONDON NEW YORK CALCUTTA

swiss arts council
prohelvetia

This publication has
been supported by a
grant from Pro Helvetia,
Swiss Arts Council

**PAP
TAGORE**
www.bibliofrance.in

The work is published
with the support of the
Publication Assistance
Programmes of the
Institut français

Seagull Books, 2020

Originally published in French as Philippe Jaccottet,
Taches de soleil, ou d'ombre
© Éditions Le Bruit du temps, 2013

First published in English translation by Seagull Books, 2020
English translation © John Taylor, 2020

ISBN   978 0 8574 2 791 5

British Library Cataloguing-in-Publication Data
A catalogue record for this book is available from the British Library

Typeset by Seagull Books, Calcutta, India
Printed and bound by WordsWorth India, New Delhi, India

CONTENTS

Having mulled over the possibility, for several years now, of destroying the thirty-odd school notebooks from which I drew the three volumes of my *Seedtime* series, as well as *Observations and Other Old Notes*—not out of any concern about discretion, for they are far from constituting an 'intimate diary' but, rather, to prevent the posthumous divulgation of the repetitious or insignificant passages that they inevitably contain—I've decided not to exaggerate my retrospective severity and to gather what, all the same, seems worthy of publication. Whence these 'Safeguarded Notes', and by selecting them I hope not to have yielded anywhere to the indulgence with which old people, as is well known, can be stricken, alongside their too many other ailments.

(Needless to say, that a brief image of their French publisher, Antoine Jaccottet, while still a child, appears here fills me with joy.)

Ph. J.

Grignan, October 2012

1952

. . . Try once again; otherwise, nothing will hold. But this movement is no longer *natural*; we know too much, collide with too many things. Those dreams in which we vainly try to climb too-steep slopes. Well, even so, let's start out all over again from the bottom, with tears in our eyes, our heart bigger than its cage, our ears closed to all outside enticements and innuendoes. A moment should come when everything becomes clear. But the slightest noises distract me, especially the most familiar ones.

(30 September)

1953

Gathering one's thoughts: they keep wanting to scatter. An image comes to mind: the movements of the rider bringing his horse to a halt; it's the stopover at the inn, the salutations on the double staircase, an image into which converge memories of my once-beloved *Three Musketeers*, echoes of Lieder, and, naturally, Gustave Roud's Jorat region. What a beautiful gaze in the eyes of the man making the stopover and slowly appraising a space that has at last become motionless! What beautiful thoughts of rest, similar to haze.

(17 February)

1957

How the moon appears, in the evening, above the rooftops. Someone shy, unassuming, coming forward only at the very last moment.

Flowers at night.

Flowers under the spraying water, their deep blue. Revealing what might be secret within us?

(1 July)

André du Bouchet's poems, like windows brusquely opened onto the landscape in full swing.

(16 July)

A young German soldier, who knows the end is coming, writes in his last letter from Stalingrad: 'The Führer had firmly promised to get us out of here, and we believed him just as firmly. I still hope for this today, for I have to believe in something! But if it's not true, in whom or in what can we still have confidence? And in that case, I'd have no more desire for spring, for summer, or for anything else that gives us a zest for life. Dearest Greta, for my entire adulthood— a little less than eight years—I believed in our Führer and his speeches. It's dreadful to doubt . . .'

This is the starkest cry of a man handed over to the revenge of the contradiction; and no less than imminent death in its most atrocious visible form was needed to make this cry break out at last.

A voice patient in its scruples and its hesitation, an uneasy voice that would like to gain ground over the terrifying silence not by beginning with a clap of thunder or a rumbling of drums but, rather, by reducing the silence, little by little, by means of brief experienced words—such a voice, today, takes more and more time to be heard; it is audible only in fewer and fewer places, with an authority that seems to decrease proportionately; undermined by this threat, the voice becomes more and more dubious, and the thunder evermore tyrannical; all this resembles the battle of a few candles in a cyclone.

Hölderlin once wrote the following to his young half-brother Carl, to whom he liked to express the best of his beliefs (it was 1 January 1799, and he had first shown, with an admirable force and clarity, the gravity hidden by poetry beneath its mask of gameplay): 'And first of all, let's make our own, with all the love and seriousness that they call for, these great words: *homo sum, humani nihil a me alienum puto*; may these words not make us superficial, but true unto ourselves, clear-headed and tolerant towards the world; yet the verbiage apropos of affectation, exaggeration, ambition, bizarre qualities and so on, will not keep us from fiercely struggling to attempt, rigorously, delicately, to bring an ever-freer and deeper cohesion to all that is human in us and in others, be this in poetic fiction or in the real world; and if the realm of darkness threatens to burst forth violently, then we will toss our quills under the table and turn ourselves over to the grace of God wherever the threat is greatest and our presence the most useful.'

This is a problem of commitment that I have not resolved: indeed, where does the violence begin when darkness bursts forth? It should be clear that war is meant here. When the French Underground movement got organized in contemporary France, many of the least bellicose and the best writers also rushed to where they were most needed. Being dangerous, the task and the fighting were no less simple for them; the enemy was visible and the kinds of fighting imposed on them. But after that? In my mind, the question remains open.

(26 October)

A violent, almost unbearable, nightmare. For a mistress, I had a rather vulgar young woman, 'of low birth' I might have said, yet a very decent gal (which I was soon going to explain to the police superintendent, fearing that he would hold this liaison against me, but he did nothing and even gave the impression of understanding). Then, coming back from a trip with my sister and going into my room, in a sinister apartment building with an inner courtyard, in a big city, I find this young woman lying on her side, a knife stuck into her neck. After asking my sister to stay there, I rush to police headquarters; it's night, and my greatest fear is that something bad will happen to my sister during my absence, whence my haste. I pressure some office employees, who are joking among themselves as in a novel by Kafka, until the superintendent arrives; I tell him the whole story. We are back in the apartment building. In the caretaker's lodge, a very old woman is standing and we are trying at all costs to get her to leave because she cannot keep herself from urinating everywhere. (I think: 'Too many calamities!') And my anxiety is as intense as ever.

Later, I see the dead woman slowly getting up; I see her face with its swollen cheek, her slow movements in the half-darkness being only a feint (as in Clouzot's *Les Diaboliques*). With my fear at its height, I awake.

Then, during the night, having cuddled up against my wife, who is fast asleep, I sense the fragility of the membrane separating us, protecting us from terror, tortures, crimes. I think of the tortures occurring everywhere at this very instant. And I tell myself that all the images I have managed to forge in my writing were merely to protect me from all that.

(13 December)

1958

Cala Ratjada

The harsh night.

I hear a woman weeping in the night:
what miserable work poetry is,
changing tears into stars
instead of drying up the source.

Towards 3 a.m., the droning motors of fishing boats can be heard.

Later, roosters crowing: shrieks of distress, deathly shrieks. Then evermore numerous shrieks of birds; like glass marbles rubbed against each other in the palm of the hand, shrieks as if from frightened, doomed creatures who have been grouped together.

I wanted to vomit out all human ferocity in a single flow.

During the night, truth is the daughter of the night.

(26 April)

Apropos of poetry: the essential and the very mysterious element is that there is one way of saying 'mountain', for example, which reveals (behind it, in it?) something like Being, and another way of saying the word that cannot do this. More specifically: Being seems to be perceptible where there is the least amount of 'poetry' in the formal sense of the term; that is, rhetorical figures, metaphors, ornaments. Sometimes, during these past years, it has seemed to me, and I have been struck by this, that some expressions of the simplest facts were the summit of poetry. Like these two lines by Bonnefoy: 'You took a lamp and opened the door, / What can be done with a lamp, it's raining, and the sun is rising.'

These two lines provided the most beautiful moment of the book for me. I might almost have wept with joy about them, as with some musical inflections. How is this possible?

('Andromaque, I'm thinking of you! That little river . . .' is another example that came to mind at the time, without my even remembering what Baudelaire writes afterwards.)

Two elements are important here: one, the absolutely pure and smooth tone; two, these themes involving everyday life, innerness, and no longer the epic. A nevertheless hesitant and threatened solemnness. Why solemnness? Because there is a necessary respect, a reverence when facing human grandeur—which unquestionably exists—and graveness in front of suffering. Why hesitant? Because of our weakness, our doubts, our fears. The mysterious contradiction is this: to my eyes, the extreme force of the real world, its haunting, nourishing, marvellous presence; warmth or tepidness of the sunlight, the sea in turn calm and aggressive, the profusion of life, the movement of the days, the trees, the sky—this insane prodigality, this complexity as far as your eyes can see, this beauty as well, once one stands back a bit, this order despite everything. And, on the other hand: that all these forces, all this abundance, that this reality so present, so powerful and so indubitable, is nothing but fumes on another level. Whereupon the greatest monuments, even the Pyramids with their millenniums, are mere *butterflies* immobilized for a moment in the dust. This is what is extraordinary: so much presence, so much innerness in such an abyss. Whereupon, no need to make noise: even the repercussions of the lives of Napoleon or of Alexander are but the noises of cicadas in the trees of Time.

(5 May)

What is beautiful: in a few words, in a given, precisely situated setting, to suggest space, or great deeds and human passions, suddenly opening out to infinity. For example, in *The Odyssey* when Ulysses, weary after talking so long in front of Alcinous, turns his head to the sea and waits for the sun to set, because he will be able to leave as soon as night falls.

*

Stars sparkling over the sea.
A great din of arms, of hooves.
Facing this gold, the high shadow of the woods,
haughty and bellicose alliance.
Between two fronts, I dwell in a cool shelter.

I stand back when facing the vast air occupying all of space from the depths of the sea to the peaks of mountains dry like straw.

High noon blazing from one end of the world to the other.

Stars made of straw.

We, inhabitants of embers, how can we keep on breathing?

In the cool house where nothing moves across the walls except the reflections of the fire, the shadow of dark horses, the gentleness of the alliance.

The night rises and intensifies to dispel all those appearances of wealth. At the same time as its calm steady step, the earth's smoky haze advances. Everything is but glassware and light breaths. Armies scattered, vanished, great speeches muffled into murmurs, uniforms swept away into the abyss; the camp gone, the shouting of captains sloughed off with the back of a hand that can almost no longer be seen on the quiet terrace. The insolent banner has been rolled up; through the whole universe, nothing but the regular movement of rising smoky haze.

The heedless, heedful darkness.

A whole fleet swallowed up by the smoky haze.

Too-ambitious world, your monuments carry no more weight than a butterfly hesitating between stars on which to annihilate itself!

A perfume has more force. I see a lamp and the hand bringing it from the table to bedside.

(8 May)

The idea of death has suddenly become very remote, a grey smoky haze. Any complication would be out of place here. Is it the spirit of the Mediterranean? The simple force of sunlight? Camus's *The Stranger*? No, it has nothing to do with that. Too many stylists seeking to use fine words in literature; Camus, or Mauriac, or Gide—how many others! Yet long live Claudel in this respect, his hearty peasant's health, his big heavy footsteps.

(10 May)

Among so many others, this admirable line by Baudelaire: 'The familiar empire of future darkness . . .'

The ardour that can guide us to the unknown, the at-once hoped-for and feared darkness. What was initially a rather picturesque painting or a ballet scene ('Gypsies on the Road') is suddenly absorbed, invaded by, the immensity. Yet for that, there is no need to break off the verse, to let one's voice swell: it suffices to be possessed by the depths of the vision and to know how to tune those four words.

(16 May)

'This quiet roof, where the doves walk' is doubtless beautiful, even admirable. It's the tamed sea spotted between the trees. But I see still something else, something different as well from Saint-John Perse's ample waves. I feel infinite space and the force of the water, a single line along the horizon, and always this blowing by of the air, its great movement. Little by little, I hesitatingly enter a world that was long foreign to me. It seems to me that everything has taken on an increased intensity, that the luminous veil floating over the Drôme has been drawn aside, that things have gotten closer to each other and been fortified; the obscure threat as well. That power nourishing the depths of the sea. Tender and hesitant figures—efface yourselves and leave all the room for this almost-motionless pressure, for this glare so intense that it almost becomes black!

Sometimes the pine-covered mountain scintillates as if water were trembling in its vegetation; it gleams like a green fire; but neither the word 'water' nor the word 'fire' is suitable here. All the earth gleams with a quiet force. I look at the world, I see the force of its leaves shining, the afternoon light sputtering. The time has come for a bright, light blaze. (But all this is still badly expressed.)

At dawn, when there is but a single star above clouds already tinged by the invisible sun, a last bat flies around the house and vanishes like those ghosts who, it is said, are scared away by light. Soon there will be only big birds with white wings above the shimmering water.

(21 May)

Beginning with the very first pages of Cowper Powys' great novel, I read: 'There are moments in almost everyone's life when events occur in a special and curious manner [. . .] Another peculiarity of these moments is a sensation as if there were a spiritual screen, made of a material far more impenetrable than adamant, between our existing world of forms and impressions and *some other world*, and as if this screen had suddenly grown extremely thin'.

Indeed: so many writers today will have revolved around this experience which, for the poet, is at the centre, at the source of everything!

*

Rocky cliffs. In some places, they are like the sheets of paper in a bundle strongly squeezed by a powerful hand; like the pages of a book under a printing press, before the binding is put on. More often, in the greatest disorder, dug out in all directions by the sea, bored through, knocked about, broken up. Between the movable gleam of the water and the fertile tranquillity of the earth.

Rather limp succulent plants; other plants, on the contrary, so dry that their roots look like dead wood. Big agaves on the rocky cliffs along the shore. In the forests, other plants thornier than barbed wire, and thick, dark-green bushes. Plants that resist wind and quiver only at their outermost extremities. The earth, in some spots, is pink.

(22 May)

Yesterday, the health of our little maid's father, whom we had hoped would at last be able to get up after four months in bed, worsened. She breaks a plate, then a bottle of detergent; she's crying and tells us why. We tell her that what she has broken doesn't matter and that she can go home whenever she wants. Yet at this she straightens up trembling, probably full of anger at herself, at her weakness, at her tears! Perhaps she will have hated us for a moment, because of our compassion, or simply because we saw her giving in, for such a very short while, to her worries.

(23 May)

Artá. In the Sant Salvador Chapel, to which one climbs by means of a majestic stairway flanked by tall cypress trees—as in the garden of the March Family in Cala Ratjada—red wall hangings, large paintings with historical or religious themes, burning candles behind the altar, several women praying and the fragrance of jasmine; another woman is heading down the steps, all the while telling her beads. From the top of the hill, the village is very beautiful: roof tiles darker than they are in Provence—a dark-grey-pink colour. The walls themselves are also rather dark, and all around extends the admirable greenery of the countryside, surrounded by hills. A leaden afternoon. In the deserted marketplace, a pigeon (?) in a cage, and two of those infinitely elegant, white, light-brown spotted dogs from here which make one think of Anubis. Old jalopies, dust, a few very noble mansions. An almost-sinister solemnness seems to weigh down heavily on all this, far from the good-natured torpor of Provençal villages. Something that has been lost, or has survived, or remains out of touch; a kind of dark, shiny dream.

(27 May)

Noise of the sea at night: drums mutely beating in the rain.

(2 June)

. . . I then made a kind of choice, without anything definite about it. Like someone who decides to live in a house, gets deeply attached to it, yet refuses to consider it as the only house possible and as his eternal dwelling place. Simply stated: a house where daily working and nightly dreaming tend to welcome in what is marvellous in life; but also a house as fragile as glass and doomed for destruction: 'But do not attach your heart to this temporary shelter', would sing, if I remember correctly, courtesans in a Japanese Noh play. And that this house wouldn't be closed; that we would leave it sometimes; and that a simple lamp would brighten it, a simple fire warm it in winter. Indeed, I imagined a poetry that would be like this lamp for our heart, with no ambition of rivalling the brightness of stars. But I also wanted that brightness to remain perceptible, beyond the windowpanes, at the right distance, like a promise making space grow accordingly. Mankind needs this narrow dwelling place, on the condition that it is permeable to vastness. He cannot bear being lost, defenceless, in what is unlimited; but he also wastes away when he is unaware of, or rejects, what is unlimited beyond his weak wall. It's a very simple matter: not so much intelligence, knowledge or even virtue is necessary. Nothing but a fair and fine evaluation of things. Such is the price of our breathing. Poetry has taught me this. Today, what is unlimited rages and many houses are in ruins. Even more attention is thus needed, and that love be rallied by a tender, humble detachment. This could be a path.

(3 June)

Meister Eckhart: 'Listen to me. I beseech thee through the eternal and perpetual Truth and through my soul: grasp the *unheard-of*. The Deity and God are as distinct as heaven and earth. Heaven is thousands of miles higher. The same is true of the Deity with respect to God. God becomes and goes by.'

(4 June)

Here for our love no need of a house. / Suffice the fire of flowers, the flowerbed of Time.

Meister Eckhart once again: 'Time prevents us from attaining the light. Nothing is more contrary to God than time. Not only time, but even adhering to time. Not only adhering to time, but simply the contact with time. Not only contact, but the simple fragrance or taste of time.'

(5 June)

In Capdepera, the Corpus Christi procession.

All the potted plants have been brought out onto the thresholds; three altars, one of which is especially lavish, have been raised in front of the town hall, and below them the ground has been strewn with oleander flowers. In front of the church and a few houses, pine branches two or three metres in height form big hedges, and it's very beautiful. All the inhabitants have put on their most beautiful clothes; the young women are dressed up as if for a ball. Policemen in parade uniforms flank the Blessed Sacraments beneath a canopy, a rifle on their shoulder. Someone whispers to me, with admiration, that the poles holding up the canopy are made of gold. Initially, only drums can be heard, as if for a funeral march. Then, intermittently, music played by brass instruments, slowly and solemnly. Men are carrying big candles; as in our burials, the farther they are from the front of the procession, the less solemn are their facial expressions; some of them even visibly bothered or wearing ironic smiles. At the windows, Spanish flags, curtains, bedspreads. All this lasts a long time.

(6 June)

The bird of the day, singing at high noon behind the lowered slatted blinds, above the lovers in bed.

(12 June)

Reading Bounoure, *Marelles sur le parvis* (Hopscotch on the Square).

He dares to speak, referring to Valéry, of his 'fundamental vulgarity': 'his poetry was the end of everything'.

'In fact, we don't know whatsoever what poetry is—not even lovers do. But in this realm of anguish and ecstasy where our ignorant misery is making no headway, perhaps poetry offers us a chance to get a few steps ahead, to bring some of our potential into play, aimed towards an impossible end.'

In poetry marked by historical events (he is writing about the Second World War): 'The elements of the epoch are transposed into a weightless incandescence that opens onto the divine.'

[Recopying today, in October 2008—a half-century after those beautiful months spent in Majorca—I find this language almost 'too beautiful' for my tastes.]

(16 June)

A violent sirocco blowing these past few days. As if we were living amid constant thunder. Headaches, nausea, a woman vomits on the pavement, our legs feel like jelly. The sea invades the beach, becomes yellow, greenish, ceaselessly starting all over again. It's never anything but wind, yet what power it has over our bodies! The Wind of God, which no longer blows in our churches. However, one must imagine human beings given a much tougher time by God than by this intolerable moist wind blending warmth with cold.

The rain on the big grey sea, water mixed with water. Long rain clouds over the expanse of water.

(19 June)

> *Will I sleep today like a blind man or a dead*
>   *man?*
> *Will I sink into the sterile spaces of dreams?*
> *A low drumroll beneath long stints of rain:*
> *the sea has broken into my house, the sea in the*
>   *shadow of its night.*
> *Its force and freshness are for long nude legs.*
> *The door was shattered, all my pathetic*
>   *weapons*
> *tossed to the ground, scattered, changed into*
>   *tears of joy!*

(25 June)

The sea in the morning: a table covered with crystals, with glassware. Will we ever be allowed to see a more beautiful expanse?

The marvel of this glittering all the way to the end of the world is that it is a fire of water, a cool blaze; each time, in every place where light touches water, these cold, dazzling sparkles are born, as if they were stars seen in broad daylight against the background of a clear sky.

(30 June)

Colours: the soil of harvested fields, sometimes pink like cocoa powder; the two green hues of the carob trees, depending on whether their leaves are young or old; the yellowing meadows and especially the gold of the harvested wheat and the gold one sees in the middle of the threshing floor, in the evening, when the sun no longer shines; honey within honey . . . And yet it is something completely different.

(29 July)

The highest poetry, as I wrote in *A Walk under the Trees*, is frugal with imagery (similes and metaphors). There are many similes in Homer, and of unequal value, but they are not overabundant.

I am rereading the admirable ending of the Eighth Chant, which consists only of battle tales and of dialogues on the earth and in the sky: night has fallen on the Trojan camp, where Hector has ordered that countless watch fires be kept burning all night long. It is at this point that Homer decides to compare these watch fires to brightly shining stars, when the air is windless and the remote horizon opens out, in such a way that 'the shepherd feels his heart filled with joy'. The simile thus deepens the tale, associating it with the highest figures of the cosmos which seemingly also pacify it; and the simple real detail that concludes the chapter— 'The horses stood near the chariots, eating white barley and spelt, and awaiting the fair-throned Dawn'—seems a moment in a perfectly simple, infinitely solemn ceremony. The very kind of scene in which Homer's genius has always been recognized.

*

. . . Walking peacefully in this garden, seeking what would be the most beautiful, the most calm, the most constantly light and luminous words that could be said in honour of the world, in honour of man's eyes that look at it for a while and then close and seemingly never retain anything of it . . . What I claim here I will not disavow: it seems to me that nothing has yet been said* about these vast, lively, limpid expanses, about this peace mixed with war, about these wings beating above rusted weapons . . . Nothing that would be both so vast and so barren while remaining simple and alive: something resembling a Gregorian chant.** Almost

---

* Rereading this note in 2008, I noted in the margin my astonishment: ??

** ??

always, excessive complication seeps in through such-and-such a rift: the scholastic structure in Dante (one of the supreme models, however), baroqueness in Claudel, Satanism in Baudelaire, underhandedness and moaning in Verlaine, a bizarre spiritualism in Rilke. To be truthful, I don't know exactly what I'm dreaming of. It can also apply to Saint Jean of the Cross,* yet without his firm reference to God; less those arrows and admirable flames than a man's footsteps borne along by a potent harmony in which shadow would nonetheless not be absent, far from that too-fluid sliding along into which I almost always let myself be led. An extreme *aeration*, yet ample and almost solemn, almost 'the footstep of a god', without ornaments and without officiants. The height of the difficulty, of course: a triumph that is not one, a flight that does not leave the earth, a scale of measurement that would encompass the unlimited. What form should it take? It is nearly impossible for me to say, but sometimes I happen to sense inside myself this almost-divine respiration. Would it be insane to wish to translate it into words? Perhaps I will learn the answer from those mountains on the horizon, from the progressive simplification of the landscape as the eyes gaze ever further, first perceiving the water streaming over the flowers and plants, then the

* well, well??

24

infinitely varied foliage diversely stirred by the wind, then the motionlessness spreading over what lies in the distance, that movement of looking whereby the eyes ultimately peer all the way into what is imaginary. Words, like flowers, nourished by the streaming waters, and our very life bound somewhere to the lowest places, to horrible unfathomable depths with their buried lividness, yet also fed by a kind of freshness and suddenly responding to the stars by delicately blossoming into the shape of a rose, or a star; suddenly dispersing a colour, a fragrance, in which the shadows and errors of life also nonetheless take part. The mystery of all things that rise from the earth, more or less with difficulty: flames, fan vaults, domes, vases, crowns, rockets, stars. Mystery of the multiple, of the uncountable. Dark and seemingly taciturn trees: cypresses; trees so close to wind, feminine allies of the wind: acacias; privets surging forth from the earth with tranquil resolution and ever dripping wet, reflecting light; poplars and willows given a silvery sheen by the companionship of waters. How not be astonished?

The mystery is also that the words were sometimes found and that, instead of concealing the world, they revealed it. Almost everything that human beings say, and what they do, conceals the world.

I would like to be no one but a man who waters his garden and who, attentive to such simple chores, lets penetrate inside him this world in which he will not long dwell. The bread of the air.

(12 August)

At night, butterflies dressed in dust, concealing their splendour under beggar's cloaks: this is how Ulysses, disguised as a beggar, returns to his palace, even as it is said that some gods take on impoverished forms to visit us; or little owls, big bark-coloured owls, beasts of winter, of snow, whose flying resembles ghosts going by. When night and the order of night reign, when its great outer space is unfurled; when the reality of the vast outer space appears, when the haze is reabsorbed, when man, by dint of hiding beneath the mask of night, changes himself and shows himself truer, more tender and more ferocious, grasping, ungraspable. These travellers pass through the air, silent or almost so, dressed in felt; and dreams are also in the air, unforeseen possibilities that the thunder of daylight will scatter.

(16 August)

Another beautiful moonlit night. Awakened towards three o'clock in the morning, I go to the window and with surprise discover Orion above the eastern mountains; completely to the west, the moon hidden among the black leaves of the acacia and, like a lake of milk, fog over the Eautagnes Marshes. Since the minor stars are effaced, the constellations are all the more visible: Pegasus almost at its zenith, and Taurus below Orion; Pisces, the Pleiades, and a big planet, Venus or Jupiter. Orion like a sign of snow and winter in midsummer. Dogs barking, scops owls hooting, shrieks of barn owls. Not a breath of wind. One cannot avoid, for whatever reason, the words 'diamond', 'crystal'.

(27 August)

> *. . . He's running, he's running towards the game amid the growing trees*
> *with his head so round that his legs are unsteady.*
> *He's serious even when he laughs, and when he's playing he says he's working,*
> *still light-hearted he's running to some hazy horizon,*
> *he has big eyes for facing the stain he's still not seen,*
> *he'll probably live in a world worse than ours.*
> *Will he recall the fig tree, a young woman*
> *who always said no when he said yes;*
> *will he keep a memory of the light,*
> *tears, the love of that woman who bore him?*
> *Often so little remains, and one doesn't know which ones*
> *were vain, which ones burn like wax in the heart*
> *and are carried from place to place, a procession of glassware,*

nightlights, constellations of long-lost things
that will still shine in the confused thoughts of the
old man.
We dispense gifts and refusals almost randomly,
no longer know if we should speak to him of angels
or fairies,
as for me, it's not angels that I remember,
but a bush of peonies bathed in rain,
warehouses in the valley, and prison towers;
no magic needed to be added to the streets and
streams . . .
Provided that he doesn't forget how to inhabit the
earth.

*

. . . And loves, will I speak of them without shame?
Was there a single one that was selfless, caring
for the other, prodigality and not appalling base
needs,
cut short by hotel mirrors,
or a way of holding in the hand to get some light,
the torch of hair as soon ash as tossed away?
I couldn't speak to anyone any more
of those shadows,
but I know of birds that their sleep awakened me,
I still hear their savage shrieks, but the voice
no longer reaches me, I've not changed,
I've not been wounded by the kisses of these
shadows,

and of those light clothes ripped off by panting,
all that's left is a flight of feathers
from one wall to another of the long night . . .

*

Thunder, fragrance, feathers. Shadows going by
and headlights in streets in ruins
faraway lightning like swords in the forests,
scattered debris of amorous quarrels or conversations,
scoldings, whirlwinds of snow, stars, tears. . .
this disorder of dreaming, is it the midpoint of
     my life?

(12 September)

Blazing, like the sun before nightfall: before the snow-
fall, the earth blazes, shows off its riches. The same is
true of autumn flowers: their pomp, and their death.

   A barn owl found dead on my windowsill, on an
October morning.

(4 November)

Paulhan writes in *Le Clair et l' Obscur* (The Clear and
The Obscure): 'Must one speak of God, Truth, Reality?
Why not? However, not one of these words does
not call for its opposite. Perhaps one should say, like
some Orientals, *this*. But one will think, instead, of
Aristotle's mysterious phrase: "The soul is all that it

knows." Or of Spinoza's maxim (that Hegel will repeat): "The order and the connection of ideas is the same as the order and the connection of things." At the very best, such are thoughts which one attains in flashes and which one cannot defend, but from which, once they have emerged, unfurls ad infinitum the apparent world with its brightness and its night, with its jewels and garbage.'

(5 November)

1959

Strangely tranquil chirping of the oriole, as if with detachment; while I am pulling out weeds.

(15 June)

Dream. Through the window of the family home, in L., between the branches of various tiered trees: the sunset. I am surprised and just as soon secretly worried: five or six concentric circles are forming around the sun going down, each of them a different yellow-brown colour. I am first struck by astonishment and admiration, exclaiming: 'Indeed, this is a phenomenon shown by an image in my album *Merveilles du monde* (Marvels of the World); it is exceptional and I am delighted to see it.' I show it to my mother, but my anxiety must have persisted beneath my marvelling, like a basso continuo. I look on avidly. What I see is a desert of unbearable light, from which the sun continues to stand out, as well as a star; perhaps the branches of the tree are still visible in the foreground but they are hardly real in this bright fire. I take a sheet of paper, I quickly write down—swept off now by a gust of despair—the words 'star, desert, sun' and 'this is all, it's impossible to say more', or some equivalent remark. Nonetheless, up to now, my marvelling at the beauty of the phenomenon had mastered my fear. A more precise scene will make everything worse. I now discover, on my left, some very tall buildings, and everywhere else the growing fire—like the inside of a oven, with in the foreground a red-and-white bus whose back end collapses *as if it were melting*—which must be the case. Frightened, I retreat to the other end of the apartment, as far as possible from the ever-increasing and approaching heat; in the bedroom that I have reached, I see almost in the same glance a child—my son—draped in a black cloak that makes him look like both a penitent and an owl, my mother wearing similar clothing but even more frightening because she is taller and older, and my wife prostrated in a lethargic bad mood. My mother wishes to rub a cream, which she has been told is protective, on the little boy's legs. I try to tell her that any gesture is henceforth vain . . . and I awake.

Perhaps the real catastrophe will not last any longer and also end by waking up?

This is the unobserved foundation of our lives: buildings that melt, mountains that collapse, a world absorbed by a sword-like light. What can be set against that, what kind of clothing, what fireproof wall? The ornament of a beautiful verse? All this stupefies.

(23 October)

32

The soil turned over by the plough is shining, like a sowing of broken glass. Incessant flights of yellow leaves at eye level. The sky dazzles, the wind blows hard. One begins to see the dark wood of the branches and the trunks.

(30 October)

Clouds like peonies in which daylight is gathered, whereas everything that I still see of the earth is almost dark.

Lingering at the edge of the paths, as on the streets below the walls, shreds of old tapestries.

Wealth is concealed in the darkened foliage.

(18 November)

1960

'And unto the angel of the church of the Laodiceans write.'

I wonder why these words of the Book of Revelation—the Apocalypse of John—have struck me so, ever since my adolescence when I was still reading the Bible with a blend of fear and veneration. To be truthful, up to now, I have never tried to understand them; they formed, instead, a sort of magic formula whose power depended on their strangeness, as does, in fact, all of the Book of Revelation. I didn't wonder how it could be that Saint John had to write to an angel, nor who this angel was, nor where Laodicea was located. And if those words have always remained in my mind, more than have two analogous exhortations, 'And unto the angel of the church in Smyrna write', 'And to the angel of the church in Pergamos write', then this is probably because at the same time, towards 1943, in the middle of the war, I had read Roud's short book titled *Feuillets* (Pages), of which many passages had become intimate for me, and that Roud cites this specific sentence with respect to his own 'tepidness' as a poet, even as he elsewhere quotes from Mallarmé or Rimbaud. (This also proves that in French-speaking Switzerland, the Bible hadn't completely stopped accompanying our thinking.)

This sentence thus affected me like a musical air that haunts us without our really knowing why, or like some verses or sentences: for example, later, this by Chateaubriand quoted by Arland in his *La Consolation du voyageur* (The Traveller's Consolation): 'We thought we were hearing that nameless bird that consoles the traveller in the Vale of Kashmir.' It is also a magic sentence, which has not come to mind here by chance, because it stresses the word 'Kashmir' in the same way as that other sentence emphasizes the word 'Laodiceans', that is, the Asia of our childhood daydreams, an almost completely imaginary land whose power over me will have been, back then, of an incredible intensity. There were those engraved images in the Hetzel edition of Jules Verne's *Michel Strogoff*, with their captions: 'He came to take a breath of air on the wide balcony . . .'—this was about the tsar—or: 'There was movement, excitement . . .' commenting on the Nizhny-Novgorod Fair, which would come to mind much later every time that I would listen to Stravinsky's *Petrushka* . . . (And there's no doubt that, for me, that Russia was already the threshold to Asia.) In the same way, yet earlier in my life of a young reader, there were other captions, those of the illustrations in my children's edition of *The Thousand and One Nights*; such as: 'Prince Hassan was the first to shoot' or 'The princess appeared on the steps of the pool'—images and phrases that must have had, on my child's mind, a power greater than most of the events of my young eventless life and surely than all the lessons at school. I'm quoting them now, in jumbled fashion, because they are more or less magic formulas, more or less lacking meaning and importance in themselves, yet all linked to the Orient. Of course, during those years, I also read stories about Indians, trappers and Black Americans; most of those stories probably bored me; in any case, none of them had that aforementioned charm. However, I did not yet know that our civilization was born in that Eastern direction; I was hardly aware that the sun rose there. This is probably because, deep inside us, two kinds of reasoning sleep, one historical and the other astronomical, and both feed this vague nostalgia. Moreover, it matters little that we'd run the risk of being disappointed if we went today to Samarkand, Smyrna or Nizhny-Novgorod: the real cities were not at stake, nor abstractions; but, rather, what has emanated from those names in human consciousness for centuries and which carries as much weight for our inner lives as the land registry of those places.

However, the verse from the Book of Revelation contained a special mystery that resulted from its context; first of all, from the French title of this sacred book, *L'Apocalypse*, a title which, so I initially thought, like many other people, meant a catastrophe, a cosmic catastrophe. The Apocalypse was the story of a disaster so great that it had to be told in veiled terms; it was the end of the world about which the astronomer and popular-science writer, Camille Flammarion, had provided me, at the same time, with more 'scientific' imagery—and I would later discover that the same images from *L'Astronomie populaire* (Popular Astronomy) had equally struck Bonnefoy and Du Bouchet. Finally, the Apocalypse was Saint John on Patmos; and I know well that if, later, I was fascinated by Hölderlin's poem that has this title, it was precisely because of this title, even before I had read it:

'Thus I was speaking
And quicker than I had thought
A Spirit then swept me away, far from home,
To where I'd never dreamt of going.
 And in the twilight of dawn the shadows
Of the forest grew
As we flew
Over yearning streams
 Of my homeland, then countries never
 known.
But soon, fresh and bright,
Secretive and through a golden haze,
Vaster with each step of the sun,
 And fragrant with a thousand mountain
 peaks,
You opened up to me like a flower—
Asia!'

That vast name, which burst out there like a note from a trumpet, or like a star surging forth, after which the flight (of the mind) neared Patmos—

> '. . . I was grasped by a great desire
> to go down there and approach
> the dark cave . . .'

—until that day when I discovered the sacred island in one of Hieronymus Bosch's paintings, in which the whole landscape, with its deep background and illuminated by those very depths, like the face of the saint, reflects an extraordinary kind of waiting.

And if I now read Father Boismard's 'explanation' of this book, in the Jerusalem Bible, I can again measure the destructive power of commentaries. Nothing remains of the Apocalypse if one removes its dark and gleaming veil which, indeed, envelops any 'unveiling', and every sentence thereafter appears mere remote, old-fashioned, childish gibberish. For me at least, the truth is still the sonority of this verse—'Unto the angel of the church of the Laodiceans write'—which is really as if God had pronounced it, as if there were still angels, fully alive churches and an Orient where only the sun, in the morning, would be born.

My protestant education has prevented me from confusing angels with winged muses, nor with those little cupids, those *putti* visible on Raphael's unbearable* religious paintings. I never wondered back then

*An adjective which, some fifty years later, I would no longer let myself use (2008).

what they were nor even if they could exist. But this is not what matters; images are more powerful and, as images, angels will at least have, to my eyes, intermittently existed. They were first revealed to me by this sentence—'Unto the angel . . . write'—an angel whom I knew was neither pink, nor chubby-cheeked, nor suave; but who was at least as big as the sky, that 'firmament' not firm enough to keep itself from ripping apart, opening up or quaking in its foundations; the angel was linked to the star Wormwood that flooded the earth, and carried coupes or a sword as can be seen on Tarot cards—such as I had seen when I was a young child: those greenish bludgeons, those golden coins without an origin, those crescents of the moon; and nor did I forget them; or else, the angel would put an extremely long trumpet to its mouth, a trumpet of the kind that can blow down walls and not at all one of those instruments that are played on Sundays in villages and that make one smile. Without my ever having thought about it, an angel was 'something' that was very big, as tall as the sky, and that could shatter the framework of the sky. Or the angel carried a reed—like a contemplative man, a Chinese wise man or even a stroller along the bank of flowing water—but with this reed the angel would measure a city as beautiful as a jewel: 'And he that talked with me had a golden reed to measure the city, and the gates thereof, and the wall thereof.' ('And he shewed me a pure river of water of life, clear as crystal, proceeding out of the throne of God and of the Lamb.')

(8 February)

> *In this bush of birds Time's footsteps that push*
> *away the boughs.*
> *Birds, tools of the day, creaking cogwheels of*
> *March.*

(7 March)

Back home from Paris with the night train: before reaching Dijon, a kind of small valley which, under the irregular moonlight filtered by the many fluffy, fleecy clouds, seemed to be a sleeping park, softly docile to a meandering stream, with meadows, hills, slender trees along the water. A beautiful fortified farm; and, in the two rooms of a small neighbouring house, the lights were still on, even though it was later than one o'clock in the morning.

(14 March)

One of the highest peaks ever reached by poetry is doubtless this passage from the last canto of *Paradiso*—which André du Bouchet introduced me to, or taught me how to read better—where Dante compares the brief moment of total 'oblivion' that enabled him to have the vision of divine essence to the twenty-five years of a similar oblivion that had gone by since Neptune's astonishment at seeing the shadow of the Argo passing above him: 'the quest that dazzled Neptune / when Argo's shadow sailed above him'— with the malediction for the translator that 'Argo' rhymes with 'letargo', thus ensuring to this extraordinary parallel the sonorous solidity of its echo.

(8 April)

Dream. A tall, slender young woman on the threshold of the house, amid the snow and darkness of a winter dawn; she complains that no one wanted to open the door for her. With a reproachful tone that I cannot understand. My mother gets up and slaps her, shocking the neighbours who come running. The young woman falls down, in the grip of a kind of epileptic seizure. We try to defend ourselves with difficulty.

This scene had been preceded by a walk in a city that perhaps resembled Rome, a place so beautiful that I told myself that life was definitely worth living. A castle, yellowed walls, old rounded cobblestones— under a big sun.

(21 September)

Dream. We (I no longer remember who) get into a car in the mountains. Yellowed grass in the pastures, as in winter or spring. Suddenly birds attack the car, but we manage to get rid of them. But the anxiety remains. We spot a woman-shaped boulder standing in the grass like a menhir. We come closer to talk to her. (Of all this, my memory was immediately vague.) Subsequently, the stone-woman is with us in the car; she explains that only a man's love will be able to break the spell. We respond that remaining a stone and waking up only now and then, as with us, would be better for her since she would be able to see the future centuries. Then, as we turn around, we see missiles, satellites and red stars glowing in the sky—all luminous signs. After which a flock of big black birds with powerful beaks flies back down on us: growing anxiety wakes me up.

*

Roosters crowing, wherever: calls for help.

(1 October)

Winter landscapes, the image of peace. The mere image, the mere dream of peace are beneficial. Big long motionless clouds.

(4 November)

The beginning of winter: white frost at dawn, mist on the windowpanes. A nasturtium has entered the moist cellar, with a sunbeam, through the wire netting of a small basement window. The tranquil sun.

*

Landscape of mirrors, of broken glass.

*

Faint light, pink clouds above the forests, colours of hunting.

(7 November)

I inscribe your name on the grass or the waters . . .

Winter of mist, of mirrors, ghostly sun.

(A. d. B.)
You go through the day, it goes through you
You read in the sky the harrow or the plough
I watch you progressing among the stars that are tears
And you bury them in the earth

Winter of ploughing, of clods of dirt
Grey season, dusty wind on the golden colours . . .

Inscribe the name of this passer-by in the grass
A stone would weigh down too much on his footsteps

May he be bound only to the dew
May a brief flash of light be a broken stele for him.

(9 December)

The world ever-deeper than the eyes can see.

(26 December)

(to H.L.M.)

Words effacing thought
and hiding the mouth that uttered them
to better show the dawn in the air
words to open the years
to make winter come into bud

(28 December)

1961

Go by: don't stop the light for too long,
Turning around would gather the clouds.
Mere hesitation would disturb the expanse.
'Cover your tracks' is the stream's advice.

(28 April)

A few more haikus, selected and translated by Blyth:

'Having lighted a candle to the god,
On the way back,
The voice of the deer.'
    Shiki

'Wild geese coming down,
Their voices one upon another,
The cold of night increasing.'
    Kyoroku

(28 April)

'The morning glory;
In the faces of men
There are faults.'
    Issa

(25 May)

'In the misty rain,
The rose-mallows
Make a bright sky.'
        Bashō

(30 May)

'The leeks
Newly washed white, —
How cold it is!'
        Bashō

(9 June)

'Reaching the gate,
The bell of Mii Temple
freezes.'
        Issa

(10 June)

'Going out to call back the cruican-seller
He was not to be seen;
Hail began to fall.'
        Bashō

(24 June)

1962

Having read Hölderlin's *The Death of Empedocles*, I am surprised—all pretentiousness aside, which would be ridiculous—by the kinship of one of its themes with that of *Obscurity*. Empedocles' despair, Pausanias' sad astonishment. Empedocles lost his 'poetic happiness'.

(13 March)

It's not true, he thinks, that the beauty of the world could one day grow silent; something invisible, as if behind the wall—or someone?—would nourish its secret. I don't know who is going by, behind this ivy-covered wall, and if I have really heard footsteps; at least I understand that this soft breath of air that once again seemingly scatters the thought of death, like blossoms dropping from the tree in which they had gathered their fragrances, has not come from me. Not from me, but from the invisible relationship between me and this uncertain shadow; from the impalpable and perhaps impossible link between the impalpable and the impossible. Who knows if I didn't suffer from being free in this way and if I'm not actually happy today from sensing this link, the mark of this leash on my neck? I no longer go where I want to go, for doesn't going wherever one wants to go mean not knowing where to go? I stop in the high grass, astonished by it and the flowers it hides. I smile at having found again in this world a force that easily triumphs over thinking, and I'd like to thank the season whose law I have once again acknowledged—after a period of doubt and bitterness. Is this light dazzling me, is it opening my eyes? I believe that I don't have to ask myself these questions, and this is why the light is shining. So many things will respond tomorrow to the hard rain falling today! The dark earth, the earth which will receive us, which gathers in the rotting, how it opens up, how it cracks apart right now! What a strange and shadowy factory our mind looks like when it makes a song out of misfortune. The golden oriole flies off further as I progress beneath the oak trees—as in ancient fairy tales; for a single instant, I perceive it as a plant that can fly and sing. The paths are suspended between the fields and the forest like galleries (and I think once again of those that lead to sacred caves somewhere in China).

On one side I have the sky, to my left the sky, the street in the distance, in what opens out; to my right is the house of trees, the house of holm oak, with its windows and its inhabitants, those birds similar to lamps. This is how one walks between the secret and the avowal, the withdrawal of shadow and the risk, and this double possession is beautiful.

(1 June)

Mirrors and glances. Fire. Intersecting thoughts from which fire blazes up, the invisible ardour. The secret blows on the flame. In the visible world there is separation; in thought there is no longer any; the fire blends and hides them. They falter, hidden in the fire. They are no longer surrounded by anything but their ardour reflected on things, landscapes. They are burning like the air. Their own existences have lost all importance: they are now worshippers of fire.

This is how they circulate, carried away by a tireless breath, enveloped in their burning glances. Great indifference arises in them in regard to anything that is not of the order of the wind, the fire, the elements. In this, they go back through vast distances of time: the phoenix and the salamander could once again be useful as emblems. They thus now form—were they indeed separated, disconnected—a single bird whose feathers would be flames—flying at the level of the low branches of a forest. They also resemble little meteors during summer nights; they contemplate them and recognize their own signs in them. The night reveals that their flame has grown even more.

Coolness and ardour blended, combined. They return to the elements. Closing their eyes, they become more and more like the wildest beasts. Their bodies sprout talons and fangs. Even from afar, they can guess how sweet cruelty can sometimes be. They will have—who knows?—an eagle engraved on their rings, or a falcon; because of their fast flying and their vast orbits in the sky.

*

Peonies, roses, snapdragons, fleabanes, marigolds. Peonies make a moss of crumpled petals burst out of satin envelopes. Those mouths of the earth—that one smells instead of kissing. The earth's way of speaking, by more or less orderly explosions of colour, deployments of circles, stars, swelling spheres, and sometimes formations of no less frail but more complicated edifices: pavilions, caves for powdered divinities or for emblems. Furs, tongues, lips: but, always and everywhere, an absolute candour. Like an angelic exaltation of the mysteries of the body, of the most secret movements of love.

Irises grow randomly in an enclosure of high grass—mauve or dark purple—having emerged from their silken papers among their hard green blades. Or those, yellow in colour, which grow in swamps and canals. And those little low flowers—yellow or rose—that cling to rocks, boulders, which act as fur coats for them: soft, fat, and warm, modest and tenacious.

On the contrary, in the high grass, flowers which lose their petals as soon as they are brushed up against; docile to the slightest breeze: like these poppies on long stems, the epitome of fragility, brief little pavilions, ephemeral, for a popular fair, decorations for a village.

In any event, it is always a party, a celebration, a form of approbation: never a refusal, never a tear.

They are in equilibrium for a mere instant: before collapsing in clusters, or spindling upwards, or unfurling, or opening completely out. They are also multiple, scattered or wasted—ill defended— similar to those little proclamations which are dispensed more or less everywhere and many of which will never be read.

(5 June)

Birds above us, far away, that tell of distance; they say: here is the forest, here the stream in the forest, the valley that meanders upwards, that becomes more and more distant from us as it rises; they say: beauty is visible, but distant, we are its voice, its flight, and I would like to listen to them, to follow them; they say: beauty doesn't belong to you, but it watches you and smiles. Above the forests, their song is remote, but clear.

At night, the song of nightingales like a cluster of water.

(15 June)

In the cradle of the night, the hidden flowers sag and shiver. Whoever guesses what their life is has an urge to laugh and completely forgets death. And similarly when he muses about all those plumages, in invisible nests, sleeping and sometimes swelling because of a breath of air; likewise, about the grass lying down, stretched out, or about the unbound waters. Thoughts, however, which circulate within the darkness with the night birds; thoughts that would have golden eyes and furs of snow, dreams that hover, that hunt—no one knows anything about this except those who are not sleeping: wild, agile, burning hot, avid animals, while all these flowers, these plants sleeping and breathing in the bed of night.

What is the fruit that you touch at night? The very one that will never be named, never picked, never savoured. How weightless the night is around what cannot be kept!

(19 June)

Cherries that swell, loading trees all the way down to the ground. Clouds that grow pink, in the evening, then silvery. Swifts flying fast against this tender glowing backdrop.

Flowers, almost all pink or red, why? Their resemblance to flames, yet their freshness.

During the night. The constellation of Cygnus, especially the wind, like the noise of a waterfall. The light thundering of long-range aircraft. A cricket. The dark embellished night.

(21 June)

All these birds, in flocks or alone, are soaring around in circles, diving, flying up again: what is the force that makes them inhabit the air? They chirp 'here, here, here', and this 'here' is never where one is. They are arrows whose target keeps moving, moving away. They are linked, however, to the idea of an inaccessible rest. They chirp incessantly at that moment when finally they will be—never—in the cradle of the forest, in that nest that cannot be seen—the nest that they dream of and that time refuses them.

*

Broom plants: the roads seem ever narrower, the houses farther away, soon there will no longer be anything but mountains, no shadow, and family deaths.

(10 July)

1963

Roots—under the earth—hidden, and they must not be exposed—but without them no flower opens its eyes, its wings, lights its fire. Looks brought up from who knows what centre of darkness, from what nest, from what hearth. Efflorescences. Coal. Centre of the night that opens, that blossoms into a dawn of lips. Wild animals that come out of the thicket at daybreak, fast, shy animals that flee with tiny shrill cries—still so close to terror, or to blindness.

*

A tapestry in shreds, or rather in the process of being woven. Its elements: flowers, birds and fruit.

(26 January)

1964

The tale of the battle of Salamis in Plutarch, *Life of Themistocles*. There is a grandeur there that still moves us despite the enormous changes that have taken place over so many centuries. And rereading these pages, one better understands Hölderlin's dream when he was writing *Hyperion*. Xerxes on his throne of gold, surrounded by secretaries assigned to write down every phase of the battle, and a deserted Athens where the dogs are howling for their missing masters.

*

. . . I am searching for words that can stand the test of this stone. How to find them? Look at all these shells, these shattered bits of bark, fit only for burning. I must search, not for words but for what in me is not yet shattered, or might not shatter if I collided with the stone, not in thought but with all the force of my persistent life. Surely too-glorious or too-cheerful words would then fail me, leaving me with only a very few words. Opening outwards would then become the only possible movement, and if I restate this too often, this is probably for want of being able to make this movement. Nothing but the hand speaking instead of the mouth, a weak, trembling hand ready to flinch, making a wing-like shadow against that too-bright light that looks more like a blade, like steel. The effort of this hand today, and tomorrow if necessary, and until its imperceptible shadow cannot stand it any longer, as if one were armed with a mere leaf, or a fan. There might thus still be a place in us that had been spared by the fire, one single place!—for a single shadow of word until the end.

During this blinding, unbearable opening outwards, amid this brutal evidence which is screamed from all sides at once and which seemingly can be heard screaming from farther than the depths of the world, as if the universe had caught fire and there were no more land or air: who would still wish to plant a plant, with nothing but tears to nourish it and guided by a sort of poignant maniacal attitude? Who would say 'distress' as one would have said, less near the end, the word 'joy', as if it could still be a caress or a gift?

Despite everything, something is going on, going from the leaf to its shadow, from the hand to the shoulder, from the mouth that is speaking to the ear that is listening, even if the leaf and the shadow are trembling so strongly and if we know that destruction is coming up from behind and closing in all around. We do not live in a world in which it is possible to adore only the shadow or only the fire. When this hand reaches out to help, or merely to shelter, to shelter a fire for a moment, a gesture that appears so derisory, the hand actually does something more that is not easy to grasp because the act belongs to the realm of what cannot be weighed or calculated.

Worlds exist with their overwhelming masses, their implacable movements, their calculable structures. Enormous chariots seemingly fit only for embellishing night with their trophies while they crush us. We can hear their squealing axles. And on bodies shattered by their invisible wheels, the marks they leave are only too apparent.

There thus exist those enormous spaces, the weight of mountains, those insurmountable distances, those destructions of stars, and the Law which, until now, keeps on annihilating. But measuring our life on such scales would have no meaning; nor, likewise, would claiming to ignore them. There exists another realm, indeed specifically that of the hand, of seeing, of speaking. If the two realms are compared, the power of the former makes that of the latter seem inevitably derisory and certainly useless, if not deceptive. The slightest human gesture immediately seems stricken with pointlessness, and our entire life futile. Yet we sense that this cannot be the case. We imagined the immortal soul because we became aware of these two different realms, of their incompatibility as scales of measurement. This is because we thought we had noticed, in the world, what seemed to be unusually luminous points of light; or seeming gaps in the continuity; breakthroughs; other forms of bonds, knots, and calculations: what were called angels perhaps in times of a greater boldness of the mind—what surged forth as well when two gazes met.

We translated what we had experienced as strange by putting forward that the soul would not die, as if no assertion were insane enough to make tangible what is enigmatic and extraordinary in gazes, in speech. Yet we also sense that this assertion throws us off the track and hardly convinces us. It is impossible to pronounce it as we would any other assertion from which simple consequences would follow. It does not belong to the kind of truths that solve problems. Yet if we do pronounce it, we quickly feel guilty; we would hesitate to instil it in a child, as if there were something shameless about it. How to untangle these presentiments?

On the one hand, we cannot help but view as too naive the idea of a human being surviving in his distinct character traits; on the other, the idea of a return to the common Spirit, whatever it is, has something too abstract, too mechanical, about it. What we expect, deep down, is not the fulfilment of a fairy tale, nor our integration, or re-integration, into some cosmic equation.

Murmurs, sighs, wounds, gazes: this stitch-work of our most genuine fabric seems to set something else against the scale of the universe. 'The soul attached to the body.' What does this mean? Could what would be freed or torn away from the body merely be what we call 'spirit', a sort of ghost? We sense that this cannot be. However hesitant we might be, we keep a little firmness inside us, like foundations. Every now and then, we touch them. Facing the immensity of worlds, it would be futile to raise up a wall covered with formulas, or with illuminations. If anything can escape the annihilation, then it must be some kind of passionate power—passion is not necessarily noisy or frenetic—but of an entirely different realm than that of the 'outer' power; and which perhaps has a very simple name that has, however, become unpronounce-able in the meantime.

The power to join, to leave the self . . .

A consequence: that no *formula* ever suffices (which, moreover, appears in the true philosopher's insistence upon never mechanically entering a system in order to better learn how to think, and in the special rela-tionships between master and disciple that are envis-aged, notably, by Zen, if I have understood it a little).

Whence the worth and the special truth of poetry, which rejects all formulas in order to transmit something more like *bits of energy*, and to create openings or passages, from which it follows that poetry would ultimately be less deceiving. We could therefore believe that there is no progress, since poetry apparently reiterates ever the same thing in a sort of perpetual looking-backwards. But this is because there is a motor behind poetry. In a certain way, poetry would maintain the possibility of the impossible as it is also expressed in mythologies, dreams and anything immemorial seemingly buried inside us.

Evidently, the realm of number and quantity has progressed; almost all human beings devote themselves to it today. But this apparently has its price: increasing distress. Tremendous expenditures of knowledge—and money—are used to launch into the unknown explorers who carry up there only an empty boldness and the seeds of heightened distress. Inevitable conquests, sometimes surely useful yet also dangerously insufficient. Other people maintain something else which does not have to do with conquest, which is almost the opposite of it and thus seems more and more derisory. But if one does not maintain it, isn't what is best in life threatened?

The big question for those who stubbornly keep on writing: How to make words stand the test, how to write so that words contain what is worst even when they are luminous, gravity when grace bears them along? I too often tend to dissociate one from the other.

Impatience overcomes me in front of so many detours and standstills. Neither treatises nor sermons! Let me be thrown to my knees, on the ground, be shaken! No way to fall asleep, once and for all, in order and security.

Those who manage to write an extended narrative, so many pages per day: archivists, chroniclers, accountants . . . As for me, I once again lose the thread every day. Perhaps, especially, when I seek to grasp it? Would it be better to open the door, go outside, make a fire, rake, weed? Sometimes in the same moment of living, I feel both fullness and emptiness, nearness and distance, an opening and the wall, yes and no. Words for the dead, even if they can no longer hear? No conciliation is possible. Can one speak of an ordeal without having experienced it, of war without having fought in one? Imagining is not much at all: it's easy, it doesn't bleed.

Modesty, instead. Not everything can be grasped in a few words. Simply say: at one moment, I will have seen this—the pure, open, light world; at another moment, the world turned crimson; at still another moment, the world rots and horror overcomes you. Nothing more.

(24 January)

Readings. Tieck's marvellous tales that express so well the fascination exerted on us by Alpine landscapes, their dark forests and the looming mountains.

The attraction of the *mine* for so many German Romantics; and like Hoffmann, or Jean Paul, they still speak to us with a genuine voice that remains close to us despite the distance, thanks to the humour and the fantasy that tempers their effusions!

Storytellers who knew how to retain the spirit of childhood. Comparing their world, through chance reading, to that of Plutarch or Saint-Simon is to measure the incredible distances between the climates, the lifestyles, the interests, the dreams and the infinitely various perspectives.

Still other worlds if I try to approach Plotinus or Meister Eckhart. The power of constant concentrated experience and thinking, the heights that they attain that we cannot follow.

A moral doctrine of the positive minimum, rather than fragments of negativity. Even from this minimum, we remain at too much of a distance. 'Patience and time as it goes slowly by.' No grimacing and weeping in front of the mirror; moreover, the mirror in which the writer constantly observes himself has been removed. To observe oneself, even with a cruel lucidity, is too much.

(6 February)

Dream. I awake oppressed from a dream in which Alain Borne was involved and which began with an article in the *Dauphiné libéré* about his death, which occurred the same day as a murder in the region; whence some suspicions against him, about whether he had been overcome by insanity before his death. I go into the building where he lived, I am again going to see his flat (which has no relationship to reality), I remember the first dinner that we had there (no less imaginary). Round the table, we speak of him; one of the guests asserts that his priest-friend was in the process of converting him (a friend who exists no more than anything else), etc. All of this is without any great interest, until the moment when, Alain having come back, we evoke a radio show that Radio Lyon has devoted to him; he is among us but it is no less *after his death*; he even indicates to me the people who could best inform me about him—notably, a woman who lives in the house; all this seems natural to me, there is a river flowing nearby, and I tell myself that he jumped into it. 'Then' I leave him, and the dream becomes very beautiful. As if Alain had lived in a rather poor, almost rural suburb, I walk along a path bordered by thick underbrush and sometimes brambles that cling to me. I wonder if I am not a little drunk, I'm afraid that it is too late, I cannot be sure what time it is, fearing that my watch cannot give the exact time—my watch shows only half-past eleven which, nonetheless, reassures me a little. In front of me, an oppressive landscape of mountains, one of which has a pyramidal shape; and I am not surprised that Alain had felt himself transported there to the Mexico of *Under the Volcano*; this dark terrifying landscape; but also very beautiful.

I have the impression of being lost; I enter the courtyard of a very old house, or farm: dilapidation, strangeness. When a woman notices me, I feel obliged to ask her my way—for Neuilly; this question reassures her, she replies that it is nearby, which greatly relieves me. Then, once again, she (a very old, short, wrinkled, wizened, rather little reassuring woman) looks hard at me, observing my temple and, to my question about the anxious astonishment reflected on her face, responds: 'But you have the vein . . .' or 'I am looking at your vein.' To reassure her, I explain that I have probably eaten or drunk too much. An awakening with a start.

*

It is still night, but suddenly I hear a first bird chirping, a first sonorous rocket. Sound of water on pebbles. I don't know which bird thus sings first—the doubt-dispeller ('Who hasn't heard it? But you've all heard it, haven't you?—that little bird on the edge of dawn that heralds the birth of a world as pure as its song?') I remember by heart Roud's words which I heard more than twenty years ago and which, with a few others, brought me into the heart of poetry. Against all the systems. Here I am at peace once again, outside of all the knots of dreams.

The world of poetry—and this song.

(28 February)

[Apropos of the poems of *Airs*:]

. . . One is taken up by the concern of filtering and of not filtering too much. The limit beyond which purifying means sterilizing.

Marvels exist, rottenness exists, horror exists. No way of getting out of that. This is what we poets can oppose to rottenness without denying it, this is the 'why' for which it seems we were made.

Let's take account of what still exalts in the most simple life.

Those moments that make the contours of time crack. And of which too many lives are deprived.

One maintains something all the way into the dilapidation.

(16 June)

All those scholarly, prestigious, sometimes truly superior poets impregnated with culture. They speak of myths, structures; they increase the number of words about words and about silence; and me: agedness, fright, uncourageous acts, etc. I cannot see beyond daily pains and joys. (Well, this is not entirely true . . .)

(8 September)

At the Maeght Foundation, the flowers of the lotuses and especially of the caper bushes—marvellous flowers with their long and supple purple stamens. Later, in Bandol Zoo, the crowned crane with its shivering grey-feathered fur; the macaws coloured like flags, gnawing away at the bars of their cages; the strange red-billed blue magpie from the Himalayas, as if dishevelled; the pitcher plant that looks like a pipe with a cover for swallowing insects. What most struck our daughter, who is five years old, was the little fennec, although it was one of the least strange of all these wild animals, a sort of small fox or even little dog: it must have reminded her of a stuffed animal.

The bill of the toucan seemed to have been painted by a very good abstract artist, capable of using very refined colours, although of the most vivid, gay and fresh hues.

(15 September)

1966

Back from Switzerland. My father-in-law died on the morning of the 9th. I'm going to try to note down exactly my reactions to this profound ordeal. We had a great shock in November 1965 (or 64?) when we found him in bed, ill and reduced to so little. Already at that moment we judged him to be doomed, I had seen him as a doomed man, full of distress, inaccessible. This time, because we were prepared, the shock was less. We had been told that he was very serene. Two or three days earlier, he had conveyed his last wishes to his wife and son. Accepting death, apparently, with resignation and courage. Courage he had had to the limits of a kind of patient heroism. However, I think that he was racked with an infinite sadness; even if he joked with his nurses until the end. Anne-Marie and I had admired this resignation, but also measured this sadness. (He had avowed to a friend—not to family members—that his suffering made him want to die.) He would say: 'This is how it is, it's the same fate for everyone, one can't do anything.' When he saw me, he simply said: 'You shouldn't have taken the trouble.' That's all. He didn't speak of the children. I had the feeling that he was already far away, with his pain, with his extreme lassitude, with his disgust at any kind of food, any smell, and with the thought—perhaps itself vague—of death. I don't think that he was afraid at all; but I imagine that he found it to be very harsh. He wouldn't be waiting for a Paradise: with his great good sense, he was extremely rationalist—though never a quibbler; and he must have seen in the supernatural only nonsense. A genuine artisan, modest and good-natured, to whom one didn't tell tall tales. For a long time, he seemed to want to live, and he struggled with a mute energy. Then, he had had enough. He refused all visits by the pastor, whose words, and especially whose tone, got his back up.

In his last days, he tried to change his position in bed, but he couldn't find the force to do so; so he remained for a very long time lying on his side, turning his back to us and seeming so suddenly *small*, infinitely pitiful.

The night of the 8th to the 9th was relatively calm, thanks to an injection. At dawn, he began to recover consciousness, to become fidgety when the pain returned. The nurse on watch gave him a new injection, knowing that he would no longer awake. I heard his light moaning from behind the partition, even as one happens to hear, in a hotel, the moaning of a couple making love. (I really thought of this, even if the analogy was almost obscene at the time.) I stood up. Outside, there were plenty of birds chirping, and they continued during his death pangs. He could no longer see. His dentures must have been removed so that he would not suffocate. He had become livid, awful to look at. However, there was no struggle, no convulsions. A machine continued to run, as best it could, and worse and worse. He was no longer there. Indeed, the dominant sentiment was that it was no longer him. The death pangs lasted about five hours, with almost no changes. Then the noise became more feeble. Still two stronger death rattles. The nurse on watch placed a handkerchief near his face, but nothing came out. Then we heard nothing more. The nurse shut his eyes. She held his jaw with her hand, knotted a handkerchief around his head. He immediately took on the colour of a corpse.

The serene face that visitors, later on, admired was but a pious arrangement. (However calm the injections had made this end.) Anne-Marie could not detach herself from him, wanted everyone to see him, constantly returned to that room even when the coffin had been closed because the heat had begun to exert its effect. The unbearable odour of flowers covered the other one by invading the whole room.

For me, by no means out of coldness, I would have preferred that he had no longer been visible after his death, so strong in me was the sentiment that it was no longer him; but, rather, a stranger, or worse: something else than a human being. An effigy. All fetishism in this regard horrified me.

During these difficult moments, the most moving aspect was the boat that his granddaughter, who was not even five years old, wanted him to be given, in the coffin—a brown boat (in terracotta?) as big as a little finger—next to his clasped hands. If ever . . .

Later, it was a real comfort to discover the great bereavement of the village: nearly thirty wreaths, flower sprays, plants; and to feel the warming affection of his kin around my mother-in-law, exhausted but calm, almost tearless.

Also the sentiment of a sleight-of-hand trick that sermons do with ease, by turning death into life. Often admirable Biblical texts, but distorted by the use made of them.

The friendly old retired pastor writes a letter to the widow in which he evokes 'this sublime promotion to the eternal light', which is not without beauty; but, on the eve of an operation similar to the one that my father-in-law underwent, the pastor is infinitely more afraid than he was.

In the crematorium, the coffin is placed on a sort of bronze canopy supported by six burning torches, in the style of entrances to the Métro. Gloomy. Anne-Marie could not keep herself from watching the coffin disappear (how? I didn't want to understand) into the machinery. Burial is definitely less dreadful.

I had been very afraid of seeing for the first time someone, who I loved, dying. However, everything appeared at once more dreadful and more simple, more natural. More acceptable as well, amid so much love and humility. Dreadful is indeed all of this as far as the body is concerned, and I think that it is wise to turn away from it as much as possible. But the very horror seemed to enter (more easily than I would have believed) a natural order; to be less revolting from close up than from afar.

(14 June)

Another death. That of my uncle—and godfather— Paul C., who was hardly more than sixty. A miserable death. As a child, even as an adolescent, I viewed him as a great man. He had been a military pilot, and I had long been crazy about aeroplanes and aviators. He was a very conceited, very self-confident man who retained from his profession as a lawyer the oratory tone and mannerisms of a man of fine words; moreover, he was willingly aggressive. He delighted in driving his car very fast and couldn't bear being passed. He sometimes embellished his speech with Latin quotations, even though his cultural knowledge was superficial; he understood nothing about contemporary literature.

His wife, who was one of my father's elder sisters, a primary-school teacher fifteen years older than he was and who had not given him a child, blindly admired him. They liked to make winter stays in Zermatt where he would go skiing, and later play curling; when she was more than seventy years old, she would still dance at the balls given at the hotel and the Aéro-Club.

I subsequently realized that he was not even a very good lawyer; and his few attempts at a political career were unsuccessful, perhaps out of a lack of diplomacy. It was one of those existences of which nothing will remain. He was hardly generous, little concerned about others and very hot-tempered.

When his illness would make him lose his balance, he had to walk with a cane and would fall in the bath-tub. Probably a deep sadness overcame him little by little. He lacked everything that made the end of my father-in-law's life so respectable, even as he lacked what had given support to my father-in-law: children, close friends and the memory of his virtues.

For me nevertheless, another whole chapter of memories is covered in shadow. My holidays, indeed more or less happy ones, in their big old chalet located in Les Plans-sur-Bex. His speeches on 1 August. At Christmas, his playing jazz on the piano in the style of Charlie Kunz, who was famous back then. In the chalet, we constantly had to be careful not to displease him. To touch his tools in his impeccably kept workshop was a serious misdeed. Fortunately, there were also a few records: Maurice Chevalier, Charlie Kunz, Lys Gauty whose 'Le Chaland qui passe' I would never tire of listening to; and even Mozart's Symphony No. 40 in G Minor, which already deeply moved me. For other recreational activities: darts, bowling, table tennis. I also remember the excursion up the Rhone Valley, to the west, the noise of the torrent, the oil lamps and the candles that had to be handled with the utmost precaution; and the games of lotto.

The library was relatively rich, notably in classical Italian authors—I think that my uncle's father had taught that language. It was perhaps in that library that I read my first novels of Dumas. (I am speaking of a time that must have preceded the Second World War—and the mountain landscape that I evoked in *Requiem* comes from there.)

(8 July)

16 July, back from Lausanne, where I attended my Uncle P.'s funeral. His wife, who was wearing black probably for the first time in a long time, was suddenly showing her age. Among those attending the funeral, rather little emotion; banal speeches; a few wreaths.

My aunt offers me the deceased man's watch; and as I mention that I will have to shorten the solid gold bracelet, to the size of my skinny wrist, she replies: 'You'll tell them to pay you the value of what they cut off.' (For the funeral meal, she specified that everyone would pay for their own.) Acts of stinginess like so many others that I will have lamented in that milieu.

The end of my uncle's life must have been atrocious. He fell, loaded down with his various prostheses. My parents were not allowed to see him until he was dead. His wife continued to consider him handsome whereas my father saw him purplish and swollen up. It was whispered that he had had a fit of *delirium*.

To come back to my aunt: although she dressed at the age of seventy—to my ever-strict mother's great disapproval—as if she were thirty years younger, she also possessed much gaiety, a love of life, and courage; and a sporadic kindness, disrupted by unexpected acts of nastiness.

[Since I am recopying these notes taken dozens of years earlier, I would like to add a fact that, long afterwards, much surprised and moved me. When my aunt herself fell seriously ill, she fell into a deep coma that lasted months, even years. I learnt that my father, her younger brother, who, when she was still in good health, overtly showed only a distant, distracted affection for her, and who, like many men, was horrified by sickness and especially hospitals, went to see her very often, perhaps almost every day, until she finally passed away—while she could not have been aware of this, at least as far as one can judge.]

(16 July)

A house, familiar acts, customs, the homeland: but can all this, which Deguy and his friends draw from Hölderlin as read by Heidegger, be used as a foundation as they do? Aren't they relying more on 'hearsay' than on genuine experience? When the land registry has been ripped to shreds . . . It is surely necessary to try to put together a new one, but what will be the new unit of measurement?

*

(I have reached the middle of my age . . .)

Even the most acute pain and even the most intense pleasure are,

a moment later, mere smoke fumes; they vanish and live their lives with other fumes.

Our past as the intermingling of smoke fumes of a succession of short-lasting fires, we as a brief fire and a longer smoke fume—with air in front of us, but ever-less air, and the fire burning ever-less brightly.

Fragments that make my imperceptible trail through what is vast and unknown; piled-up firewood and gardens, garden walls, fragrances of peonies and irises, scary strolls along narrow ramparts and towers, a few scenes of arguments glimpsed or imagined as if in a hideous theatre, old ladies cloistered in the shadow that makes the high-ceilinged bedrooms seem higher, the despondency of schooldays, the figures of 'schoolmistresses' hot-tempered like big roosters, mysterious alluring places like the arsenal, the sawmill, such-and-such a remote little house at the edge of a woods; the locks of the stream, the spinning mills, the prison overlooking the stream. The despondency as well of icy mountains, the beautiful noise of the torrent flowing below the vast park full of ferns and mushrooms.

The great figures of uncles who will totter and collapse much later.

And the parents strangely so little visible, as if they had almost not existed, only sporadically—during that period of time when they were still leading their own lives, unknown to or misunderstood by us, in all events kept distant from us.

Why awake these truncated images? So vague despite their persistence, mere trifles, and no one can assert, however he has lived, and in whatever way, that he carries anything but this burden of smoke fumes— inside his lantern, in the cage of his bones (imponderable galaxy swept off in some whirlwind) . . .

(20 August)

The first morning in which the whiteness of autumn is ablaze, in the chilly air; one of the most acute and mildest moments of the year. The sky is like a pale, blind glory set upon the foliage of the vastness and half veiling it.

(25 August)

The 'devotees of language': it is a religion, an illness. Count on them to turn the Gospels into a Littré dictionary, and the crucifixion into a trope.

(3 November)

Phaedo 115e. Socrates to Criton, before the last farewells to his friends: 'False words are not only evil in themselves, but they infect the soul with evil.'

1967

Secret caves in China (in the magazine *Du*, May 1960). Some photographs of the caves of Maijishan (Gansu province) published in this issue have fascinated me as few other images have done. These caves, about two hundred in number and whose dates range from the fifth to the ninth centuries, are situated in central China, in a not-very-accessible region, which explains why they were 'discovered' only in 1953.

The mountain slope is full of holes, like a piece of tuff. In front of the caves are suspended superposed wooden galleries connected by means of ladders or inclined planes. Some are half-destroyed. The rock seems to be ochre in colour, the wood almost pink.

At no moment did I pay more attention to the statues and wall paintings of these caves than to so many other works of art that one finds beautiful without being any more attached to them than that. I know that they did not fascinate me in themselves but, rather, by their presence on that mountain slope, associated with the view of a remote landscape, with the light—at sunset—shining on them, and especially with those rundown wooden galleries and walkways suspended above emptiness, in front of the caves.

Perhaps their image was associated, in me, with childhood memories: those wooden balconies of chalets—themselves linked to holidays—that give one a sensation of well-being because of the fragrance of the wood, because of the heat stored up in them while the mountain air is crisp and cool, and because of an impression of old age and patience in which they envelop you. I wonder if there isn't a connection as well to the China of *Connaissance de l'Est* (Knowledge of the East) with the pavilion of the waterfall that I believe I also come across here: the dream of a house *suspended* between air and rock, like the eyrie of a bird of prey. And then, all the same, that vague assembly of unknown gods in the mountain who are illumined by the evening sun, who are peaceful and speechless and who can be approached only be trusting in those rustic wooden planks boldly attached to the steep wall, honeycombed like a cliff of seabird nests.

(17 June)

To read Michel Deguy writing of Hölderlin in the *NRF*, one could believe that the greatest merit of the poet would be that of his philosophical *system*. The epidemic contagion of theories. Poetic *oeuvres* that are covered with technical, scientific and philosophical terms, like so many pimples. The modern muse wears a white coat and glasses. She is a doctor who wishes to disinfect the world, both inside and out. Among her diplomas, at the top of the list: a BA in sex.

(9 October)

Towards nine in the morning, the mist clears. I go up to work in the cabin with the intention of testing the heating. The sky is uniformly blue (more than in summer?). Not a puff of wind. Nothing but birds frightened by my footsteps and crossing the path in front of me, from one bush to the other. I recognize a robin, a magpie, a jay flying off with its grating cry. A titmouse is fluttering around the house.

Even if my bodily machine sometimes happens to feel worn down, it marvels at this opal light glistening on the leaves like so many drops of water. Morning, noon, evening: from white to gold, from gold to purple. In the morning, in the east, the light is like haze. The day's childhood. Time, 'a child playing'.

The last grasshoppers, the last butterflies.

Birdsongs: a measure, several kinds of intervals— in the sky and under the trees. Also, sometimes, what seems to be a door creaking in the distance. Or the sound of a tool. Or else, the birdsongs are fierce, or frightened.

(20 October)

Events. How is it that the wonders of science and technology—especially the exploration of interplanetary space—seem to exalt no poets, nor anyone? Why do we understand that Hölderlin wanted to celebrate Christopher Columbus and that it seems impossible to celebrate the cosmonauts? Why did Char, for example, write his 'poster' against 'the man of outer space' ('a billion times less bright [. . .] than the granite-like man [. . .] of Lascaux')? Russian youth seem prouder of such feats, but is this because they have been trained to feel so? Indeed, in America, no wave of enthusiasm seems to have risen because of feats that are no less than astonishing. Isn't there subject matter here for more than any *Legend of the Centuries* or *Divine Comedy* with the idea—which is no longer unconceivable—that some of our descendants will exile themselves from the earth in order to people other planets, swarm off into the infinite and so on? Yet we have the feeling that only demagogues, with their propaganda, could touch upon these topics. Why is this? Perhaps it must be explained by referring to Leopardi and his doctrine of *illusion*. These new conquests are borne along by no illusion. No one appears to believe that they can bring us true benefits, nor, in any event, heal us from the despair overwhelming a mankind worn out by the growing weight of its ordeals and crimes. As far as I can observe in my narrow field, human beings seem weary and would above all like to *breathe*. The diffuse feeling of an almost-inevitable, at least ever-possible and realistic, catastrophe is what weighs down on them, disarms them, sickens them. If we see in our midst so many people turning to yoga or other analogous disciplines, this indeed implies that we are suffering more and more from a problem of *breathing*. While our 'material' body is exposed to sunrays, almost all of which are beneficial, our 'spiritual' body is increasingly bombarded with images, a great number of which are harmful. At best, it therefore seems that cosmic expeditions might exalt the mind as a chance to flee from a doomed world—but can fleeing exalt?

I often think of Ungaretti's pages about Michaux. It's true, never has the link between past and future—the continuity he describes elsewhere as the central theme of *The Aeneid*—appeared more tenuous, more threatened. Consequently, many people whom we know dream only of dwelling far from towns, in an old house and according to age-old rhythms of life. Like old people, we watch on with melancholy as traces of former lifestyles vanish, only to be replaced, too often, by the construction of buildings and objects that wouldn't seem so 'ugly' to us if there were not some deep reason; yet this 'attachment to the past' also bothers us. Supposing that we consequently preferred to join the party of the 'moderns', what is disturbing is that not just *one* party exists but, rather, a hundred simultaneous rival parties which, what's worse, become outmoded almost as soon as they emerge. (The above shamelessly repeats some of the thoughts expressed by Musil's Ulrich with whom I long cohabited not for nothing.)

In his pages, Ungaretti, so strong and radiant, seems to dread, not without sadness, that writing such as his could become anachronous and lose all validity because of what he senses has become, ever since Hiroshima, a radical break with the past; that is, according to him, ever since mankind has become aware of the possible annihilation of the planet itself. Moreover, he fears that the new kinds of rhetoric (or anti-rhetoric) are still incapable of fostering a genuine renewal. He thereby acutely describes an *extreme* state of affairs where nothing, neither old nor new, can re-establish the minimum of confidence indispensable to life—and to creativity.

With this position, he lets a permanent residue of Christian convictions show through; and if he has recourse to them, we cannot see that he finds them elsewhere than in *love*. But can what he thus calls *love* resist the break that he denounces? If man can no longer believe in any paradise, either 'in heaven' or on earth, yet can no longer see anything but hell every-where, what kind of life and what kind of art therefore remain possible?

In the final reckoning, the question perhaps comes down to determining whether it is Leopardi's 'thought', or his 'poetry', that is true; that is, if his *nihilism* should be adopted—and the history coming after him would only have aggravated it—or if his lamentation should be listened to when it is expressed in a poetic 'body' where, as it were, it is absorbed and transfigured; in other words, whether his completely naked, if not skeletal, thought is right or an ensemble in which thought is blended and modified—the sensitive 'body' which a poem always is and from which ever emanates less a reflection than a light, more or less limpid or more or less convincing.

(11 November)

1968

Coming back home from Aix-en-Provence on the evening of the fifteenth. The sky was clear higher up and cloudy on the horizon, with big white moving shapes that were tortured and bright, as in a painting by Tiepolo; later, when they had darkened, the clouds were full of pink lightning flashes.

Came an hour when the light of the sunset painted all the houses pink; the beautiful hospital in Carpentras looked like a Roman palace, and Vacqueyras was also still rose. Then an intensely luminous yellow was predominate among greens getting darker and darker in the Cairanne Plains; a painterly beauty was given to the landscape in the distance and I was moved by this more than I had been in a long time (despite an inner uneasiness, a kind of tension that has lasted ever since the news of the invasion of Czechoslovakia, I think). We had also seen sparkling, on the slope of the mountains, on the still-visible stone of the houses, the lights of Gigondas and Séguret. A sort of transport, or transfiguration, of all things.

(16 September)

1970

That man who embarked one day in Grignan, straight out of his Parisian suburb where he had sold, for a good price, a small house—to live here in peace, with his wife. A short man who had flat feet, a thin face and a long nose, and who was welcomed with open arms by the owner since he was a skilful handyman and, just after arriving, had enhanced the flat with a new shower, repainted the hallway and cleaned out the cellar from top to bottom. Then the owner employed him in his own flat: he liked to talk, and possessed the self-confidence, know-how and bad tastes of an average Parisian. He covered over the beautiful old woodwork with bright yellow paint, took care of the orchard and soon got involved in absolutely everything. In the village, he would give advice all day long, chat here and there, criticize, collaborate: a genuine gadfly. It didn't take us long to understand that his knowledge was not as universal as he pretended. We ended up finding him to be a nuisance; from all sides, people started turning their backs on him. During the first year of their sojourn, his wife sang as a 'soloist' during the interval of the parish church feast day, with a voice rather on key but quavering; because she must have been more than fifty years old and was neither beautiful nor elegant, to watch her singing a ridiculous song with this refrain—'I'm the nightingale of love', the entire room was seriously threatened to burst out in laughter. That was the first and last time that she performed. From time to time, their daughter came to see them; a tall girl who had remained single, had a big mouth full of shiny teeth, her father's long nose and a mane of hair; standing very straight, rather abrupt in her movements, she was conceited, especially when she was with her parents, whose mediocrity—it was only too obvious—she could not bear. I believe that she taught German; she also sang but, considering herself to be from an *entirely* different level of society, was merely an unfriendly, stuck-up, self-important woman. Her mother fell ill with bone cancer, suffered greatly and died by coming undone like a body falling apart.

The little man has remained alone. A long time ago, his stomach had been removed. His daughter is now in Cannes, where she moves, he has told me, 'in higher levels of society' in which she probably is too happy to return often to see him. He knows that all his internal organs are irremediably worn out, except his heart ('fortunately', he adds, and I'm not sure that this is the right word). Yet he increasingly has fits of suffocation during which his blood pressure goes down to 5, his heartbeat becomes 160 and 'he sees himself dying'. He can't stand being alone any more.

Fortunately, an old lady takes care of him, lets him stay with her when he is having his suffocation fits which can last for days and against which the doctor can do nothing.

For such a man, can there be any other kind of help, any other light, than religion? But if one considers religion to be a lie or an illusion, isn't this the most *absolute horror*? Isn't it from this, from a single story like this one, of which I have merely outlined a few pathetic, cruel, lamentable characteristics that are visible on the surface, that a rigorous, violent, sometimes fanatical rejection of our world can be born? Isn't this what Beckett tries to look at, face up to?

And I also know well what 'but' will follow, beneath my pen, as it has always done when I have been brought back to this point, refusing that horror contaminates all the expanse of my sky.

So what now?

(5 February)

Disgust at words.

(10 November)

1971

The acacia suddenly more white than green, laden with fast-fading clusters of flowers, with something *poor* about it, often dead branches, seeds left over from the season before, leaves of a somewhat yellowish green colour—recalling some festivity in the suburbs, cheap decorations that the slightest rain can spoil—this is why so many were used (girandoles?)—and the wood is itself easily broken (it grows fast, anywhere, with special requirements, sometimes takes on not-very-elegant shapes—nothing in comparison to the beauty of oaks, chestnut trees, lime trees). A tree for embankments, a hobo tree (?).

Partly drooping branches, and dangling clusters of flowers. Wisteria. It strikes me as strange that flowers, in my most remote memories, take up so much room. The wisteria of our friends, M., in Yverdon, before they had a villa built, which perhaps dates this memory to 1930. The word 'glycine' (wisteria) and the thing, and especially its fragrance. With a kind of beauty, surely, but also with a quality that I cannot express otherwise than with 'cheap', and not of the best taste, like some mauve scenery or ornaments, from the 1920s. Vague but intense memory, and still vaguer approximations.

(15 May)

So many things assail you . . .

The garden full of high grass, full of leaves, because of an incessantly rainy season. Those plants in the morning, when you come out of the house, at your feet: like tender little familiar animals. The freshness and the limpidity that is there. The shadows in the morning; the sky through the dense foliage of the honeysuckle.

This, indeed; and the high meadows full of flowers in the Ardèche, near Privas, and the chestnut groves.

The bad news that has come from L. The images haunting me—of my mother taken to the clinic, of her dread, and I keep myself, perhaps in a cowardly way, from being overcome by it. The degradation inflicted on old people. Why is it that God has not sometimes been conceived of as a sadistic monster? (But this has surely been done.)

Perhaps this is why I wanted to read Shestov once again (*Sur la balance de Job*, On Job's Scales).

Along with this, hardly farther from us, the worsening contagion of violence. Can one both applaud teachers who encourage their students to treat them as equals—when they do not claim to learn more from them than they can impart to them, which quickly turns into demagogy—and deplore that governments no longer govern and limit themselves to following whatever events occur?

(8 June)

Spiderwebs on the books piled up in disorder.

Efforts to make: against the little desire I have to do anything.

A strange time, changeable, stormy. As if an order had broken down. Grey light, pale sun, dusty, wandering wind. Mosquitoes. Landscape viewed as if through a grimy windowpane.

More or less remote memories, but more frequent and more present.

Natta in Florence, in my pension hotel in Oltr'arno, the painter Sadun in Sienna—and my total innocence back then, which made me go through all that: it's almost unbelievable.

My mother in the clinic of Y., like a human being who is drowning too far from you to reach out your hand—locked up in fright and unable to control it any more. Then once again calmer and almost like before.

The vague desire to gather all these things scattered inside me, to dig more deeply into them. But also these vague impulses for change, this desire for the unknown, the weariness in front of everything that begins once again, eternally identical—landscapes included. Nostalgia now and then for the big city, but the Paris that I think back on probably no longer exists. (Or, rather, who I was no longer exists.)

Shestov. I sometimes feel, probably through shallow thinking, that he repeats himself too often—that what he wishes to say could have been expressed more briefly (?!); that is: that reason has its limits and that one must take the leap beyond, under the (inner) death sentence. But the choice to 'take the leap' still seems to be a matter of reason (?) . . .

(6 July)

The spider dangling in front of the windowpane. Slowness and silence of its movements, interrupted by long pauses. It is perhaps this slowness that disgusts us. It is very different from the immobility of a fisherman at the edge of the water.

Once the fly is caught, the spider reels it in with seemingly mechanical movements of its legs, then hunches over its prey, reels it in still more closely, thus creating an entire geometry of variable triangles; the spectacle is atrocious to see. The spider, as if stumbling, finally takes it away.

(18 September)

Death of my aunt M. C., after a deep coma lasting nearly a year. With respect to her are mixed in me images of gaiety and horror. I had dreamt (the very morning of her death?) of her big chalet, in Torneresses, into which suddenly came a fox, then a cow—which later became a tall woman wearing a blue, very low-cut dress.

(20 September)

In the morning, in the garden, light haze lit up by the sun. The weather is mild.

Thousands of swallows are soaring above the houses or shivering, perched tightly against each other in rows, on telephone wires. It is raining.

Last night, hostages were killed by the mutinous prisoners in the Clairvaux Prison, with makeshift knives made out of the prongs of forks.

(21 September)

The fig tree losing its big leaves, which have become yellow, and making room for the sky. As when one opens a door, when one removes an obstacle or clears off a path.

Tree thinned, lightened.

(9 November)

1972

Visit of a childhood friend of Anne-Marie's, A. N., who lost her husband a month ago: her story.

Once again, one notes that Balzac's cruellest stories, for example *Cousin Pons*, by no means exaggerate the blackness of reality.

The harshness, the rapacity of men of money, partners of the deceased husband in a construction company, rummaging through his things even before his death, demanding that the exhausted widow hand over some of his keys the day after the funeral, ready to deprive her of all her rights, to crush her, to bribe, if necessary, her lawyer. Even taking into account the possible exaggerations of a not-entirely-stable woman, who is also too uncompromising to be diplomatic, what she describes are genuine hyenas.

In addition, another funereal comedy: that of the priests. The same building contractor (who has become wealthy through his constructions which have made the region not just a little uglier) is himself an Italian immigrant, a practicing Catholic, who has his grip—according to our friend's story—on the local clergy. A few months ago, he apparently got the young, friendly, very popular but also imprudent priest transferred; that is, probably, because of his rather-too-free look, and because he was too much appreciated by the women parishioners. The young widow, having been subjected to the visit of the new priest in a state of drunkenness, refuses to let him preside over the funeral and has the preceding priest brought back to the village; the latter accepts, on the condition that he will not have to appear until the time for the ceremony had come. The 'great' contractor, so that he will not seem to have been manipulated, gives four days off to the titular priest (which will cause some embarrassment, since another death has occurred in the meantime and called for another ceremony, whereas there was, temporarily, no longer a priest). The former priest thus hides out in the village; the carpenter, a decent little fellow with a moustache who is also the funeral director, is an accomplice. One evening, he invites the widow to his house to decide on the last arrangements; there she finds, with delight, the former priest, who comforts her over a bottle of wine. In order to go back home, she is reduced to taking the darkest lanes of the village. A strange novel.

During the funeral service, the second one of the day—because one of the deceased man's brothers, who is also a priest in the Tessin region, has celebrated a Mass, without telling the widow, with the Catholic clan—the whole village takes their seats on the side of the family of the dead man, leaving the 'big boss' and his wife, nicknamed 'La Douce', alone on an empty pew.

Our friend insisted on seeing her husband who had died from a heart attack at the age of only fifty-six. She says that she was able to recognize only his bangs. His hair had whitened in twenty-four hours, and his teeth were completely black.

After all this, she says that she is happy to have discovered Buddhism and that she believes in reincarnation. Her husband, who had known for a long time that his health gave him no more hope, had often spoken to her about Buddhism and reincarnation. He saw himself, as she explained, coming back in the form of a tree.

Both of them were simple people: she, the daughter of farmers, and she claimed to have inherited from her father the gift of curing warts; he was of Italian origin and had worked as a painter and a plasterer. He had quickly earned a lot of money—although, being more of an 'artist' and less greedy than his partners, he must have been conned by them more than once—and built a big house that he little by little filled with old furniture and old books, his great passion. Books which, I suppose, he didn't read very much but which he loved for the quality of the paper, the binding or their oldness—appreciating, like many craftsmen of his country, 'beautiful work'.

(15 February)

The songs of the cuckoo and the hoopoe are related.

The former: as if muffled, evoking a hole that would seemingly be made, in the thickness of the air, by a tool wrapped in rags, something round and opaque. As if in cottonwool? Note produced by a veiled instrument, if not muted. Ever in groups of two, while the other one is triple and faster, a triplet.

Both as if coming out of the haze. And measuring, as with all birdsongs, a distance.

The songs of sparrows, titmice: like clusters of wisterias.

(4 May)

The still-soft skin of the bride

—and the song of the bird that naming alters, which comes to you in bursts, so beautiful to rise into the darkness of the night.

(6 May)

1973

Roger Martin du Gard. Induced by circumstances to reread his *oeuvre*, to read his correspondence with Copeau and Gide in regard to an edition of his letters to his daughter, I discover a man who interests and moves me more than I would have thought. His natural novelistic gifts are so great that, while reading his letters to Christiane—several hundred in number—one has the impression of reading the story of his life as if it were a novel, to see his characters on stage: in the foreground, with his back turned, the author himself, massive, solid, but in fact deeply anguished, taking up nearly all the space; facing him, a little girl who, as she grows up, stops giving in to all his wishes, begins to rebel, and, by doing so, disappoints and irritates her father who wanted her to be perfect as if she were another of his literary works; and in the background, his wife, a sickly, pitiable, almost speechless ghost.

The correspondence with Christiane stops in 1947 after a dramatic disagreement; his correspondence with Gide in 1951, after the latter's death. Well, one wants to know what happens next, as in a novel! Especially, to know what happened to the big book on which he had been working for years, *Maumort*, and which he had not been able to finish.

To know who his last close friends were, where and how he ended his life, etc.

At the same time, I discover some interest in Gide whom I have never liked and have thus little and badly read. Having never met him, but having met some of his close friends in Paris, I often wondered what his prestige was based on. (In my Paris years, I heard people speak of rue Vaneau as simply 'Vaneau', even as I imagine that in Greece, centuries ago, the initiated would have spoken about Eleusis . . .) The lasting and lively friendship that du Gard had for him encourages one to rediscover him; as well as their correspondence, the abundance and frankness of their exchanges. I thus began by reopening *The Vatican Cellars*, a novel that I had read more than twenty-five years ago, but not well. I reacted to this reading, essentially, with the fear, expressed by du Gard himself, that the sovereignty of the 'style' might conceal a lack of 'substance'. The ease, the flexibility, the quickness of the language make one marvel and sometimes, when they turn to affectation, irritate; admittedly, the drollness, the savour, the impertinence of the words amuse; but in the final reckoning, one isn't fulfilled. I thought of Voltaire; and this comparison, pertinent or not, expresses, in any case, the limits of my admiration.

(15 January)

A story of misfortune. Liliane J., who had been such a merry girl among her sisters, all of whom were, in fact, a little wild in character—she being the prettiest—had married a big, strong fish warden who was probably a little coarse but seemed quite friendly. Everything seemed to be going well. She would accompany him, to go fishing, in the Sorgue—they lived in Fontaine-de-Vaucluse. Then they came to live in Valréas. This was where the first rather serious hitch occurred: Liliane had followed to North Africa a tax collector who was older than she was; after a while, she left him to go back to her husband, who I am not entirely sure had been absolutely faithful. The tax collector was smitten to the extent of writing to us, knowing that we knew Liliane, to get a word out of her and threatening to kill himself if she didn't comply. We replied, I think, that we refused to intervene. More time went by. Liliane, who could not bear children, was success-fully operated on by her doctor. At the clinic, she was charming and happy. The child didn't come, and he confided in Anne-Marie that she felt deeply helpless. Later, we learnt that she was staying in a psychiatric clinic because of a serious depression. She stayed there for three months.

When she left the clinic, she rang our doorbell. She was herself, and no longer herself. She went down the stairs like a robot, staring straight ahead. As soon has she had reached the room downstairs, she stretched out on the couch, exhausted from the medication that she continued to take. All of her gestures, previously so pleasant to watch, had changed, stiffened and lost their symmetry. For quite some time she stayed on the couch, her legs straight, seeming weary, absent, worried; avowing that she feared to encounter once again in Valréas the same solitude and the same boredom as before; then, suddenly, she said goodbye, as if it were imperative that she didn't linger a minute more. Anne-Marie was very frightened and downcast by this visit.

L. was again here yesterday, alone in the house when I returned from the post office. When I opened the door, I heard a strange voice staying something that I couldn't understand—which must have been simply 'is it you?' or 'you're here!', but which, in its strangeness, scared me for a second. Then I discovered her in the stairway, almost totally stiff, her eyes staring straight ahead even more and, especially, duller than the other day. Her speech was also more spasmodic. To give me her hand, she reached it out so little that it seemed to be held back by invisible bonds. 'I have stiff muscles,' she said. She had just left her doctor, who was sending her back to the clinic, and she wanted Anne-Marie to drive her there. Since Anne-Marie had gone out, I asked her to wait. She was trembling; she could hardly hold the piece of pie that I gave her, along with some herb tea. She was entirely aware of her state, and asked me if it were visible.

Then, abruptly halting at the end of every sentence, all the while looking at me with her so-strangely-changed eyes, with her mouth tensed up, without the slightest trace of the charm that had been hers when we had met her, she said: 'It's my husband . . . He is harsh . . . He says that I do this on purpose . . . He says: "I also can tremble when I want to" . . . I want to divorce, we don't get along physically, we've never gotten along, ever since . . . But my father doesn't want me to. If I divorce, he won't ever speak to me again . . .' The most distressing thing is that we wonder if, in such conditions, she will ever be able to be cured, as can be hoped by a woman whose social milieu is more stable and who knows that she will find a genuine home when she comes out of the clinic.

Once again, I wonder if a woman who discovers, when she is young, a world completely different from (and, in some respects, superior to) hers, does not run a great risk of losing her mental balance because she does not have the material and intellectual means to gain access to that world, so much so that this world, which she has only glimpsed from afar, nourishes a toxic nostalgia in her. Such as a farmer's son who, having studied literature at the university, discovers poetry, art and so on, and decides to risk his life on them, although he has few or no gifts: he loses the taste for the social milieu in which he has lived without being able to conquer the one of which he daydreams.

Similarly, I could easily tell that Liliane J. (who had visited us when she was very young when we would host our artist-friends in rather festive atmospheres, and was wooed by them because she was attractive) would think back on such moments, and that she liked our lifestyle, because she had much more sensitivity and finesse than, for example, her sisters, more than that of her family. (Her father, in the village, was considered to be a poacher, a sort of Gypsy, who was thought, rightly or wrongly, to beat his wife.) But Liliane, despite her charm and kindness, had little chance of finding among our friends a young man who would love her enough to allow her to pass from her world to ours. She thus married that simple, perhaps brutal man, all the while retaining daydreams that were more present in her than they should have been. In addition, in recent times, she had befriended a former high-school classmate of our son's, a woman who lent her books that were 'dangerous' for her, in the sense that they could only nourish and worsen that nostalgia—whereas she was fabulously ignorant and naive. This is why, once she had come across in some attic an old pipe with a Turk's head bearing the inscription 'Jacob's real pipe', she looked up the word 'Jacob' in the dictionary and, discovering the patriarch, no longer doubted that she was now the owner of his pipe. (As incredible as this may seem.)

(20–29 January)

La Chine nouvelle: a documentary film presented by a Belgian traveller with banal, but level-headed, commentary. The discipline that is as worrisome as it is admirable: masses grouped into parades, into squares of gymnasts, into battalions of workers. A beehive droning with words pronounced by Mao, on whom the camera lingers, during a session of the Party. The god whose icons are carried in procession, whose thoughts are tirelessly recited and are nothing less than seductive in form when one thinks of the beauty of the Christian liturgy; I do not know if this depends on the fact of knowing that he is like this, and so powerful, that we find him strange, tranquil as he seems to be, sunk into his armchair and making gentle gestures with his hands, slowing turning to the rostrum, slightly making an at-once-paternal and half-cunning 'good smile'—but all these words that I have ventured are perhaps completely false. The mechanical ugliness of the ballets following the traditional art of the Peking Opera.

Once again, one cannot help but admire the clear-sightedness of Father Huc, in the nineteenth century, who had predicted what China threatened to become if it found a new 'emperor'—and who jotted down so many characteristic details that are still timely: the ability to work like ants (dams built by villagers in a year), the role of newspapers pasted up on walls, the cruel punishments—thieves' hands were still cut off at the beginning of Mao's reign. 'Today, there are no more thieves.' Such statements, constantly churned out, and about many other subjects, make one sceptical. No more prostitutes either? No more rebels, lunatics? No longer a single artist, a single writer to question the pertinence of official aesthetic theories? No longer anyone to question that a writer becomes better if he does the work, one month a year, of a poor peasant?

(29 January)

Jacques Borel's *La Dépossession* (The Dispossession). This book is probably morbid, literally, but also poignant. I am indignant at the contemptuous superficiality of three reviews, by Claude Mauriac, Bertrand Poirot-Delpech and especially Michel Cournot, and so I have myself decided to write about the book.

I admit that Borel has a fascination for death, as expressed by his painful and cruel notes, taken day after day, about his mother's physical degeneration; and this fascination also affected me when I was young, though I have now mostly turned away from it. I have not been able to decide whether turning away from this fascination implies diverting oneself into amusement, that is, turning away from a 'truth' that Borel, after Leopardi, likens to nothingness, or if it implies yielding to the force of an error. However, if this were indeed the truth, shouldn't one either totally reject life, or object to this truth by putting up some, even illusory, light against it? The writer's daughter's smile suddenly casts light on a few pages of the book and thus indicates a direction that he does not want to, or cannot, take; and this is what can be appraised as morbid. Out of love for his mother, he destroys the life around him—without forgetting, on the other hand, that he could 'take advantage' of the situation on the literary level. But the mother's figure, in the way that she haunts these pages, is completely poignant; and the thoughts that he draws from their common ordeal run deep.

*

The subtlety of Jude Stéfan's poems, his masterly art. Sometimes his poetry is very beautiful, often *too* subtle to my liking. In Jean Tortel's poetry, where beauty is expressed differently, sometimes appears the risk of repetition within too-narrow limits; it is like a game of chess, played in a garden, that can make one wish for a gust of wind from outside and perhaps from very far away which would blow over the chessboard and all the black and white pieces.

(24 March)

Thinking of the piece of writing that I am working on, I know all too well what I wish I had written and from which I have distanced myself as far as possible: texts like those that Pierre Leyris gathers in his series ('Domaine anglais'); short stories, for example, by John McGahern, Stephen Crane, Edith Wharton. Yet such is completely impossible for me.

What I admire in them: the successful alloy of violence and sobriety, of realism without platitudes and mystery without fancy phrasing; texts that are neither 'literary' nor 'anti-literary', in which words are used without detours, without hesitation, yet not without art; intelligent texts without being intellectual, sorrowful texts without pathos.

When I wonder what discoveries I have made during these past few years, I almost always refer to this series. It is therefore unsurprising that I feel paralysed in front of the blank piece of paper, and displeased with almost everything that I write. It seems to me that no one in France is able to write like that— with that down-to-earth force and especially that apparent *naturalness*. Here, when the real world enters a book, it happens tumultuously, ostentatiously, as with Céline, however worthy of admiration he otherwise is. Giono, in his last writings, possesses something of this force coming from within, but he too often displays it, like a Hercules in a fair—the kind of character whom, in fact, he likes. Compared to these

English-language authors, Gracq and Mandiargues have something about them that recalls a parlour author; Dhôtel seems rather frail; Arland both too pathetically moving and too refined. Thomas, in his best books, is perhaps the only writer whom I could compare to them.

As to myself, I won't be able to shed my old skin.

(18 April)

Bad news from my mother. Will one be able to indefinitely resist the assaults, the inrush of this? And how can she have accumulated so many anxieties that henceforth they are all that seemingly remain of aliveness?

(24 April)

A book by one Madaule (a relative of Jacques?) about a book by Blanchot: despite all the admiration I have for the latter, his depth, his liking for self-effacement, the attraction that the reader can experience for the mute music of his language, I no longer have the desire to enter those labyrinths—probably because I lack the thread that would free me from them. No desire to find myself *closed in* and facing that fascinating darkness like a Minotaur who might well be born of our musings, of our hazy thinking. From those knots that can be untied in a single movement, a single step.

Similarly, while typing up a translation of selected letters by Rilke, all the while keeping intact my admiration for his poetic genius, I better understand what Kassner called his *fallacy* and sometimes irritates me by the excessive subtlety of the net in which he takes shelter and encloses himself.

(30 April)

Christiane Martin du Gard's Burial.

We left on Thursday, on the 8th, by train, with our old friend Wayland D. A change of trains in Paris, then in Chartres. The more the trip progressed, the more the train cars were uncomfortable and smoky, and the more our apprehension became acute.

André Berne-Joffroy was awaiting us at Nogent station, ever elegant but a little sunken and driving clumsily, like an old man. There was still some daylight when we entered the admirable rose-coloured courtyard of the Château du Tertre, after the *allée* with its royal and golden trees leading to it. Fernand Dubuis arrived almost as soon to usher us into the library, his complexion hardly more ashen-coloured than in September, his eyes bloodshot. When he saw Wayland, whom he wasn't expecting, and thinking of our musical evenings, he said a little theatrically but with emotion: 'You see, the party is over. The curtain has come down. No more music any more . . .'; and he led us into the parlour where a plain wooden casket, covered with a large cashmere cloth, had been placed on trestles in front of Vernet's large view of Marseille. We didn't know what to do—except not to think very much, so as not to suffer too much.

Later, Annick came in. We had dreaded meeting her, but she invited us to dinner, all the same. Pierre Viala was there. Annick is a rather astute woman, with short dark hair mixed with grey, with a still-quite-young appearance and leaning slightly to one side (without much resembling her mother, or so it seemed to me). Fernand had forewarned us that she was completely conciliating, and sincerely moved. Nevertheless, the conversation remained difficult and interrupted by long silences. The testament had already been read, so she knew of the role that Christiane had given me—partly against her two children or, at least, to ward off the effects of their devastating zeal.

The next day, the day of the funeral, the weather was admirable and almost mild in the sunlight. At noon, André Frénaud came for lunch at our hotel; he had at last forgotten our quarrel, and I was relieved. We went back to the Château du Tertre at three o'clock. Dr Dubuis and his son were strolling in the garden. Jean Limon, Annick's husband, who was a doctor, was wearing a light-coloured suit and a bowtie, his hair discreetly wavy; he was very much a man of the world and rather vapid. The wife of Daniel (who was ever living at the other end of the world because of his work as an ethnologist) was wearing a rather hippie-like dress, had a pale complexion, a perfectly icy face (which she will keep, with a sort of insolence, until the end—while Limon will take pictures of the funeral procession and even the lowering of the casket into the grave—to be sure that his mother-in-law will not climb back out?). Annick is in deep mourning, with bloodshot eyes. Then the Tardieus arrive, Jean flushed with grief while his wife's face is pale and bloated; both are very moved (they had not known anything); then Marcel and Jeanine Arland; Hélion, Auclair, Henri Petit, Berne-Joffroy, Muriel Pontremoli, Copeau's two daughters: not very many people, and almost all of them Christiane's closest friends, or so it seems to me. She had organized the ceremony in detail, as she had done for her testament, with a meticulousness worthy of her father. Recorded music rises mutely: Monteverdi, Gesualdo. Frénaud reads one of his poems, which expresses a brutality that seems out-of-place here; Tardieu, a text written for Christiane, which is of a great and touching simplicity, and he tried, until the last moment, to get someone else to read it.

Afterwards, the villagers, with Bernard, the guardian, carry the casket under the lime trees and lower it into the grave, at the spot chosen by Christiane. The priest softly recites a prayer in Latin. The words have something noble and reassuring about them, which mysteriously is in keeping with the sky that is visible, just above the grave, through the tall, nearly leafless trees.

After this, it is clear that the small group of family members, gathered in the library, are waiting only for all of us to leave. They silently recover possession of the château against the intruders who must have been, to their eyes, for thirty years, Christiane's friends. Tardieu discreetly picks up his suitcase, Frénaud cancels his hotel room and Anne-Marie and I go back to Paris with the Tardieus. We think that we will never see the Château du Tertre again, or without pleasure, and perhaps, as far as I am concerned, for harsh debates. Fernand Dubuis remains with Viala, and Wayland.

Back home now, I begin to leaf through the contents of the trunks that were delivered to me, this spring, with the terrible news of Christiane's illness. Her notes on her correspondence with her father, excerpted from her own diary; the file of the trial, with her comments; the terrible instructions that Martin du Gard gave to his grandson, Daniel; excerpts of the correspondence between Herbart and Roger Martin du Gard. One is shocked and astounded by the painful violence of the confrontations between members of this family. 'The Atreidae,' said Tardieu without irony in the train to Paris. The same conflict that so vainly and absurdly tore apart father and daughter begins all over again between Christiane and her children. The impression that I had had, just after reading through the correspondence between the father and daughter, that of a theatre setting dominated by the father's overwhelming shadow, was only too accurate. Neither had the patience to seek to understand the other; the way they all looked at each other had a vast *distorting* power. I dread what awaits me when I try to respond to Christiane's wish. But surely I must do everything I can so that her personality is less abominably caricatured in the minds of her father's readers or his future biographers. And perhaps I have myself enough moderation to obtain a minimum of conciliation.

(14 November)

1974

Two radio shows in a row, about theatre plays: Giraudoux's *Judith* and Paul Claudel's *Conversations dans le Loir-et-Cher* (Conversations in the Loir-and-Cher), both staged by Silvia Monfort. A meaningful confrontation: Giraudoux's tragedy, whose setting is noble and theme grave—the conflict between human love and fanatical fervour—makes one think too often of a conversation in a parlour of the sixteenth arrondissement, while Claudel's, somewhat similar in origin though about bourgeois characters who are travelling in France, like Larbaud's characters in *Allen*, paradoxically goes beyond the bounds of its subject matter, radiates, sounds clear and in tune from beginning to end. An extraordinarily dense and solid plotline, whereas the other play shows too many gaps. I felt joy seeing an old admiration confirmed, of the kind that, so one fears, will later turn into disappointments.

Generally speaking, it seems to me that I have suddenly become more sensitive to the *texture* of the works that I read; this is notably the case for the books, by Henry James, recently read or reread—and of which I feel the verbal, 'material' existence with as much force as the themes. The admirable 'Beast in the

Jungle', so close to 'The Altar of the Dead'. The incredible sense of emptiness, of the spectral, around which the book—grey, transparent or opaque in turn—is woven.

(11 February)

In Paris, saw Fernand Dupuis once again. He is obsessed by the memory of Christiane and by worries of her estate. He now repeats himself often, a man too alone and too old. I am far from sharing his enthusiasm for her ambitious attempts at novel-writing with which she entrusted me. He says: 'It's as good as Stendhal. Proust appears bland in comparison'—which is pure madness. Now that I judge her so little gifted for writing, how can I fulfil my duty towards her?

(20 March)

Back home from Italy. Visited my mother, who says she is feeling anguish without knowing why. Then, in the museum, the drawings by Soutter ('Moi aussi j'ai mon Gethsémani', admirable). This goes together.

Every time I see Chinet again, he is less strong and more moving.

Savoy with beautiful meadows.

(7 April)

Back home from Switzerland. My mother died on Tuesday, 21 May, at four o'clock in the afternoon, in the sunlit bedroom of the nursing home in which she had slowly declined ever since last October; through the foliage, I would hear birds chirping and the noises of a nearby construction site. When I had seen her again on Saturday, she already had the pinched nose and contorted mouth of a dying person; but, that day and the next day, she still recognized us. She could hardly formulate the slightest sentence, and groaned almost constantly, trying to sit up in her bed and sometimes managing to do so. She surely suffered from anxiety, but I am unsure that this anxiety differed from the kind of which she periodically complained. On Monday, we saw her sleeping more calmly. That evening, a new and very powerful fit of anxiety, according to Madame C., the director of the nursing home, who did not inform us at the time. However, on Tuesday at two in the afternoon, she beckoned my father and me to come immediately. My mother's pulse was no longer perceptible, her blood pressure low, her hands were almost cold, her eyes closed. When the nurse raised one of the eyelids, the eye below it was already dull. Through her open mouth she was breathing ever-more weakly, though without a death rattle. At a certain moment, my father, who wasn't feeling well, went down into the garden. I noticed that her breathing was weakening even more and I ran to inform Madame C., then my father, while making the dogs bark since they were not used to so much haste. Almost immediately afterwards, we could see her tongue hitting against her teeth, her breathing halted, took up again in longer intervals, then finally stopped without contractions or a struggle.

Later, my sister and I went back up to see her. She had been dressed in an embroidered blouse, a bouquet of garden flowers placed between her hands, and a chin bandage enveloped her bloodless face. Her mouth was closed, narrow and hard. She seemed extraordinarily long, thin and stiff, like an idol, a recumbent statue in wax, something totally foreign, by no means peaceful but rigid; something terrible.

However, at least in appearances and at the time, I felt much less shaken than by my father-in-law's slow painful death. Probably because this was not my first contact with death, and because we all expected it as the only desirable solution and, in all events, preferable to the slow decline that my mother had experienced among the other human wrecks in the nursing home. I had suffered much more the past year, when she entered the clinic and then, later, the geriatric ward; now I felt both relieved and shocked cold. But I wouldn't be surprised if this last image of her, so motionless, skinny and cold, continues to haunt me—as it has already come back to me tonight in a state between sleep and wakefulness, after a long anxiety-ridden dream in which the colour black once again struck me, the black opacity and seeming exitlessness of a big city in which I was tormented by the fear that hooligans would attack my wife and daughter, who were with me; and where the automatic gates of a subway station—gates that perhaps looked like those through which my mother's casket had to be pushed to be burnt at the ceremony at the crematorium—closed before we could leave, because my wife and daughter had lingered at the other end of the subway car; a long nightmare in which I no longer could find on the map—and still in the middle of the most funereal darkness—the name of the street where we were supposed to find a house to take shelter in and which was called—not without my immediately noticing the dark irony of it—the rue des Assassins; a nightmare in which, at the end, we crossed a dark river on a kind of ferry whose seats looked like the coloured plastic seats of children's merry-go-rounds.

*

Several days of absolute emptiness, doubtless following upon, though it doesn't seem so, my mother's death. Little by little, I am recovering. The beautiful weather, without being too hot, helps.

(28 May)

Once again, the feeling that prevails in me, after painfully rereading the proofs of my poems (*Chants d'en bas*, which will appear in August at Payot)—rereading them as quickly as possible, as if not really to see them—is that they should be replaced by something else, that this is not how I should have spoken, that I have let myself once again been misled, deluded by words, by the rhythm of the verse, etc. This is only half-true, if the movement of the verse can also, sometimes, not lead astray, but lead one where one must go.

Perhaps this is more or less what needed to be said; let's admit this, to state things quickly. But it needed, needs, to be said in a less 'lyrical' way, a less 'rhetorical' way as well. It would be necessary to speak in a way that I do not know, have never known, how to do, that is, I would need to be someone else, to change, and one doesn't change by merely giving an inner order to oneself, by making a 'good resolution', and one is probably less and less able to change. It would be necessary to be more vigilant, more severe, about the 'truth' of what one expresses, about avoiding detours, prevarication, the ruts of what comes too easily. It would also be good to mistreat the too-melodious rhythms of verse, to break with all kinds of elegance; but how can one manage to do that as well, without artificiality?

Will I thus manage to say, for example, that, while re-envisioning, in my mind, my dead mother in her embroidered shroud, her head enveloped in a whitish chin bandage, a bouquet of garden flowers in her skinny, spotted hands, and lying there absolutely straight, long and thin, that I thought of one of those gadrooned, painted Spanish candles that I once had brought back from Barcelona where they are probably used for solemn festivals, and which yellow over the years, enveloped in tissue paper, in a cardboard box? An image of which I would like to relieve myself, and which I will perhaps never chase from my mind, from inside my eyes and inside myself, so strange she was, an absolute *stranger*, mutely, icily, to the world in which, for a few more hours, she found herself placed and where there was a blue sky, chirping birds, the noises of machines and foliage, and, especially, the invisible air continuing to circulate between the death chamber and the outdoors, between the indoors and my heart, not to forget my father's wearier heart, ready to fail.

Even if I have just written that I should be more severely vigilant than ever about the appropriateness, the accuracy of my words, I must yield to images that come to me without my having sought them out, nor even expected them. I will thus also say that the white corpse so extraordinarily long, skinny and stiff was also like a knife that had been stuck into the body of the daylight, an icy blade held motionlessly by some-one who could not be seen, in any way. But not a sword—by no means!—nobly lying on a bed like King Mark's, especially not a noble, seigneurial and heroic weapon; nothing but a knife blade, that is, steel, sharp, rigid, cold, implacable; and nor is it a knife resting on a table and become inoffensive and familiar, but a blade in the process of acting, however motionlessly, in the process of cutting without any blood flowing or spurting from anything like the body of daylight, invisibly, motionlessly, silently.

And despite all this, there was the sun, the blue sky, the green trees, the noise, the warmth; which I cannot keep myself, right now, from sensing as the essential opposition with which I find myself confronted; that is, there was the pale extinguished candle, the contorted, almost bitter face, the icy knife—and space, the vast invisible air, the infinite air; this space full of life that I had rediscovered one night while walking across the garden to toss the kitchen peelings on the pile where they would mix with the leaves and the earth, while it was chilly and I was beginning once again to see sparkling through the trees the stars unbound from their familiar constellations.

(7 July)

Witchcraft. At the Trappist Abbey of A., where our priest takes me with a Hungarian organist who likes 'old things', we are received by Father X., a former opera (or operetta?) singer who arrived here rather late and who had already surprised Anne-Marie and me with his rather affected attitudes, his bizarre bird chirps and his rather confused artistic élans. As I listen to him enthusiastically making comments about the beauties of his abbey, I have the impression that I am listening to Simone Girard, a lady who was passionate about music and used to organize concerts in Avignon. In the study hall, he explains that he is especially interested in astrology, that a Chair of Parapsychology has just been created in the Vatican, and that many medical doctors come to see him because of his ability to use mind power to heal. He grasps the organist's hand, announces to him that he will live until the age of seventy-two and that he has 'great tactile sensitivity'; then, taking the priest's hand, he promises him three levels in his 'spiritual ascension'. After which, our Hungarian sits down at the small positive organ and attacks a prelude by Bach; the priest starts up his tape recorder just as soon. Father X. listens, leaning over the console of the organ directly facing me, looking at the organist. When I watch him with his eyes staring at the young musician, he makes me think of a female impersonator lacking only the make-up to be completely convincing. One of his two eyelids droops, like that of a pleasure seeker, over a truly velvety brown eye, and a strange smile is frozen on his lips. All of a sudden, the organist stops playing, having lost his way; he tries again and then gives up. It is the first time that this has happened, he says. Father X. walks around the instrument, nears me and asks: 'Do you believe in the fluid?' Surprised by the question, I vaguely respond something. He adds: 'I'm the one who made him stop. I wanted to see if I could affect his hypersensitivity.' While saying this, he smiles like a crafty maid. All the same, the organist attacked a new piece; and, since Father X. has once again taken up his position on the other side, I notice that he has also taken up an unequivocal expression.

(28 July)

Dream. Although I have been informed that my mother is dead, I am strolling alongside her on the Grand-Pont, in Lausanne, and very surprised that she is still alive. Suddenly, one of her friends, Mme G., spots us: she makes a frightened, almost horrified movement, not wishing to see her (perhaps this is related to her refusal to go and see my mother in the nursing home at the end); but at the end, they greet each other, and I see my mother placing her tearful face on the shoulder of little Mme G.

(27 August)

1975

I must have written this year at the top of the page, at the beginning of the year; then this page has remained blank until today (since the end of October, I had noted a few remarks while reading Dante).

This is because I had to translate, at the same time, two collections of stories, then Chagall's poems. The first third of the year was devoted to finishing these projects and to taking trips to polish them.

Turin was first, in the fog, between 23 and 27 January: Lucentini and I worked for twenty-four hours during three days, so that I had little time and energy to see the town. It appeared sad to me; the deterioration of the political situation in Italy was reflected in the deterioration of the monuments. Half the Sabaudia Museum was closed; the rooms remaining open were empty, chilly and dusty; the Madame Palace, beneath its profusion of eighteenth-century gilding and ornaments, was empty and the image of a world forever swallowed up, the dilapidated spectre of frivolous and outrageous luxury. But this impression of sadness resulted not only from my weariness, the season, the circumstances. The Palazzo Carignano will always have been that strange dark-brick monument with surely beautiful but heavy shapes. However admirable its cupola, the Chapel of the Holy Shroud will always have been a black marble, truly funereal, sanctuary.

Lucentini is an odd character. He lives in a pleasant flat on the top floor of an old building that looks out on the piazza Vittorio Veneto—where a noisy funfair had been set up—and is surrounded by beautiful fragments of ancient inscriptions and small paintings made in Italy by Dutch artists, like that Poelenburgh uses in *The Sunday Woman*: landscapes with ruins that all convey, in a small space, the dream of quiet harmony. His library is full of dictionaries, guides and ancient authors. As for himself, amid this: nervous, atrabilious, ferociously anti-modern and pessimistic, a hypochondriac, peremptory in his judgements, exasperated and desperate about the evolution of Italy. I have trouble understanding how this intelligent and sensitive man, surrounded by such objects, could have begun producing books as facile and meagre as the two last fruits of his collaboration with Fruttero—also a well-read man, a great reader of Valéry, who, at first glance at least, has nothing of a vulgar careerist about him. (The success of *The Sunday Woman* must have turned their heads.)

The next week, Anne-Marie and I left for Saint-Paul-de-Vence. Chagall is eighty-eight years old. He has shrivelled up with age a little; and when we walk alongside him, we sense his fragility. But his mind remains alert, at once quick and distracted, gay and sad, and the man very much likes to please, to be loved, flattered—in which, at the bottom, more modesty than vanity can be seen: perhaps, today, he is still astonished by the path that took him from an impoverished neighbourhood of Vitebsk to this luxurious house and this official fame.

In the studio where we work together (but this time, he showed his desire to finish up quickly, lost, impatient and muddleheaded as he was among his never-classified manuscripts), no painting was visible. However, the last day, as I had to return to fetch a forgotten document—and it was only a few minutes after having said goodbye to him—I found him already seated in front of his easel, very small in the corner of this vast room, near the windows; I could make out a painting dominated by white and red and withdrew just as soon, without seeing any more.

*

At the beginning of April, a new departure: for Lausanne, Vevey and Italy.

. . . In the Aosta Valley, the vine arbours made of very old grey wood were like stones in front of the stones and slate roofs of the simple houses.

In the Plain of the Po, the fresh vegetation of the meadows, the new, almost-still orange leaves of the poplars, the vast, measured and clear space at the base of mountains similar to snowy fog. I now prefer this plain, which I would have looked down on in the past, in any case looked at only absentmindedly, to many landscapes of the Marche region, Umbria, or even some parts of Tuscany, too arid for my tastes. The big square farms, the brick-pillared sheds filled with straw and closed off like walls, as well as the hedges, prairies and light.

. . . In Parma, seen too quickly: on the grass-and-pebble square in front of San Giovanni Evangelista, in the silence of the surroundings, a few people frozen as in a scene in one of Fellini's films: a priest wearing a soutane, the devout, the poor, the crippled.

. . . Ravenna, San Vitale. Once one has barely entered, one is trapped. As much as I need to make an effort in big rectangular basilicas to overcome the sensation of emptiness and coldness that they give me, here no effort is required. In the warm shadows of this octagon, in the interplay of its arches, in front of the mosaics of the presbytery and the apse, the colours have the effect of incense. By magic, notably emanating from the alliance between the hieratic quality and the almost-insane sumptuous splendour of the colours. It is like an eternal celebration and a splendour which is, all the same, inaccessible.

Right next door, the little Mausoleum of Galla Placida appears, from the outside, as modest as a garden pavilion. Inside, unfortunately too lit up, nothing seemed more beautiful to me than the garland of leaves and fruit brimming over from a basket adorning the intrados of the first vault.

I would like never to forget what blossoms in this remote place, as if suspended, asleep, at some distance from the sea. And the strange, heavy, barbarian mausoleum of Theodoric seen through an orchard of trees blossoming in the high grass, not far from factories, sheds and the Candiano Canal where big merchant ships dock. [. . .]

. . . On the way back, in Milan, at Lamberto Vitali's—who took me aside for a moment to read his poems; warm, passionate, insolent Vitali—his Morandis that are extracts of silence, as there are extracts of perfumes.

(7 May)

Celan's translations of Mandelstam, the first translations that make me grasp fully the beauty of this *oeuvre*. The admirable poem where he washes outside in the cold night.

*

Visiting René Char (for the first time, which will remain the last time) on the First of May, led down there almost forcefully by Ivar Ivask and his wife, who were passing through Grignan at the end of their European year. Both of them were always charming but with a little too much love for the word 'poetry', as others have for drinking.

Char lives a little outside L'Isle, on the road to Saumane. Driving by, one sees a vast high-grass meadow, a fortified farm, a distant blue sky beneath a fresh downpour of light. The 'Busclats' is a little white house amid beautiful fruit trees, behind a hedge of cypress trees. It seems empty, dozing. A nightingale is singing not very far away. At the end, the barking of his dog alerts Char, who sticks his head out the first-floor window, recognizes Ivask, comes down, opens the door and warmly welcomes us in. He is tall, yet now rather stooped—like an ape with long arms—with a large face as well, a big nose, furrowed features and knotty hands. Wearing pants that floated over his body, and a blue denim shirt: a sort of big gardener. His accent and way of laughing remind me of Jean Tortel. Nothing of the haughtiness that I feared but a surprising juvenility for a sixty-eight-year-old man who is ill (he has just returned from a stay in a Parisian clinic). A young woman is there, frail, slender, not really pretty, sweetly smiling—an amorous nurse. The living room is overcrowded with books and furniture; on the wall: Braque, Giacometti, Szenes, Vieira da Silva, Brauner, Denise Esteban. Canes, a decoy. Having offered to the Ivasks one of his books published by Maeght, he visibly looks around for something that would give us pleasure; and holds out one of the numbered copies of the first print run of *Le Nu perdu* (Nakedness Lost).

When we leave him, the golden evening light is already on the gravel of the walkway and on the meadows.

Back home, opening *Le Nu perdu*, I am sorry that this friendly encounter has not brought me closer to these pages and not corrected anything of my old reservations.

*

Yves Bonnefoy's most recent book, *The Lure of the Threshold*—once one has accepted the step that is necessary if one is to reach those rather solemn heights—is really a great book, with more than one mountain-born page admirable like an organ. Better than in any other of his volumes, he has known how to harmonize his daily experience, his culture and his great themes. The rowboat, the star, the fire which, in *Yesterday's Wilderness Kingdom* sometimes seemed mere words, return here with weight, density, warmth.

Similarly, André du Bouchet's radio appearance was useful—and sometimes, I had the impression of immediately comprehending texts that had remained closed to me. He reads aloud admirably well, with a kind of dry, almost raging fieriness—but always absolutely sober. After which Jean-Claude Renard, who is not without gifts, seems emphatic and talkative.

(13 May)

Of a beautiful trip to Portugal, across Spain, I noted only this:

Lisbon, for the first time—upon our arrival, towards one o'clock in the afternoon, in dazzling sunlight, at the Folk Art Museum, the Convent and the Church of the Hieronymites spotted on the other side of the road and the square, a long white line with an ornamented top; then the opening towards the estuary of the Tagus. The masts and the blue-white-yellow flags made me think of Larbaud, the white walls of the Craftsmen's Market, a silvery, translucent light, the other bank of the Tagus with its factories set inside it, its few boats, the calm water.

Then, favoured by the happiness of the moment, the surprise at the entrance to the church in front of the thin pillars, the shadow of the chancel, the cable moulding, the stone foliage—and the mossy cloister dense with foliage, as if it has sojourned in the depths of the sea to draw out its delirium of shapes.

The whole day marked by a kind of luminous inebriation.

On the way back, after the countryside around Fátima—naked soil or wheat beneath the olive trees, Tomar, that great empty and silent expanse with the crackling of the cicadas and a warmth more dazzling than heavy, where we progress from one marvel to the next.

(19 September)

Death of Saint-John Perse on 20 September, at the age of eighty-eight.

[To my mentioning of Mandelstam in *Seedtime*, page 268, were several other pages of commentary about that poem, of which the following is perhaps worth keeping:]

> What, in such a poem, could be set forth as an example: that no trace of research, brilliance, can be found; only the simplest, harshest words and things; and this tight weave, and so much space, such deep force in this narrow, special, ordinary framework—well, not completely ordinary: for is it ordinary to wash oneself outside at night, in front of that closed door (or behind it, if a gate is in question), in that coldness, and is there not in this a denunciation of the fate of a condemned man?

The use of 'great' words—abyss, delirium, ecstasy—as well as (but this has long been known), that of words supposed to be 'poetic', more poetic than others—incense, lily, dawn, harp, etc.—is to be proscribed: too many poems today abuse them ad nauseam. They cannot recover their power unless they are rare, or awakened by the use of humbler, harsher terms such as, indeed, in Mandelstam's poem.

I also notice that a rational structure, a linear development, of well-founded metaphors are quite far from weakening the mysterious dazzle of these verses. For that, no need to unchain surrealistic extravagances, so tiresome most of the time. What escapes reason in the poem does not need to be, if it is to be sensitive to us, a feigned disorder or more or less gratuitous aggressions towards reason: what escapes reason slips between the joints, between the words.

Would one perhaps need to go back to Baudelaire, to Villon, to find in our poetry an equivalent to the perfection of these verses?

(Perhaps I am also exaggerating a little?)

(6 October)

1976

In Paris, paying a visit to Francis Ponge. I arrive at rue Lhomond at noon, a little ahead of time. The front of the building is being redone: the staircase is dilapidated. Odette opens the door; she has grey hair, but her face is still so beautiful, her figure so straight and slender. Francis comes out of his bedroom in an undershirt; he seems shorter to me than before, especially a little frailer (he is seventy-seven years old); but his face has changed little. In front of me, he puts on his suspenders and a shirt while Odette insists, against his protests, on making his bed.

Like so many other times twenty years ago, I spend the afternoon in his study. After he has spoken to me of his mother and the death of his father, rather quickly, everything he says is about himself, especially his difficulties with Gallimard. I soon start feeling a headache and not without effort will I follow this long monologue concluded by the reading aloud of a few pages about the wind, which will not completely convince me. He is a wounded man. (His riposte to his former admirers, Pleynet yesterday, Prigent today, took on once again the violence of battles between surrealists.) He reasserts his Gaullism, proclaiming himself even more ultra than Michel Debré. What is happening in the world disgusts him; he even avows that he will be happy to leave such an atrocious world. When he evokes recent kidnappings of children, I discover him on the verge of tears.

He shows himself to be very harsh in regard to Perse, hardly less so with respect to Char. Great praise, however, for Maldiney (who obviously would not be able to cast a shadow on him).

My notes about Góngora seem admirable to him and bear witness to an authentic 'moral equity'; this is because he is cited as the true modern successor to the Córdobian poet. Of course, I am happy to have paid tribute to him in this way, despite some distancing that he had been sensitive to, notably in 1986; but such naive pride distresses me.

This said, the sentiment dominating me when I return to the hotel is indignation against the material difficulties that a writer of such calibre must endure.

(11 February)

Garache. This painter's reds and pinks, colours of a tender fire, of a tender nearby sun. (Yet such an aesthetic choice must not become systematic.)

It's *gathered* into a sort of flamboyant egg, or pebble, or stone; it's *concentrated* into a soft mass, as if held in the hand, picked up—or like a piece of fruit.

Nothing torn apart, provocative, showy. Both shown and hidden. The face turned aside or closed up in hair. Roundness. A dense cloud. Which shines forth softly, silently.

(How faraway that sun now seems, that warm ball. The terrible slope of ageing. I remember on the dusty stage of an old provincial theatre, that graceful will-o'-the-wisp, flexible without limpness, disturbing—a young woman also completely dressed in red, in a costume of a Shakespearean prince.)

What else could I say about that fire—while thinking of Garache's art and of the project that must bring us together? Orange. Oranges amid the shadowy greenness of the orange trees in Saint-Paul-de-Vence, last winter. Arbutus trees, fruits of paradise. Fruit forbidden—or remote.

Fire. Its relationship to mountains, to ridges. Mountain as the soothed memory of a great fire.

(26 February)

The slow steady march of clouds, some above others, those rain-seed-swollen pieces of white fruit lit up, made pink, ripened by the sun.

(10 September)

1978

A walk behind the Graillon Farm, one of the most
beautiful farms in the area because of its big barn, held
up by a strong round stone pillar and where straw
piles up like a wall, its threshing floor that can be made
out in front of it, the boulders on which it is built
and below which water flows into a basin irrigating a
small flower and vegetable garden. I cannot keep
myself from feeling moved there, as if in front of a
sort of monument, I mean something almost imme-
morial and almost sacred, something—the building,
the lifestyle—that seems to have emerged from the
depths of the earth and that now is sinking like a ship,
whereas nothing that would like to replace it seems
'true' to me. A strange, sad feeling that is, however,
stronger than any thought. We greet the old farmer
who still lives there with his son; the other son, a priest,
has come to say hello to them. Tranquillity of words
exchanged in the bright sunlight and the surrounding
silence. Dogs, sheep come into the courtyard.

(30 October)

1988

Sometimes the snow helps, as does the pinkness of a still-almost-childlike face. Snow that disappears before touching the ground. This year, snow will have struck me as being almost more beneficial than the blossoming, too early as if gone astray, of the almond trees, which the snow interrupted just in time.

*

Étiemble conversing with Pivot on the television the other evening; thus, inevitably, whether he wishes so or not, a little 'for appearances' sake', wearing his more or less Scottish-looking cap with a pompon. Of course, he appears friendly, even sometimes moving; but, if Confucius has been elected as his supreme model because he defended Truth, Justice and Freedom; if one sees in the 'well-read' individual whom one has accepted to be the man who risks being killed for having dared to criticize the prince, is Étiemble worthy of his model? The only example that he cites of his interceding with the prince, is his letter criticizing Mitterrand for having praised Chardonne. However, wasn't it that prince this time—even if skill and interest in his own appearance were involved—who established a hallmark of equity? I am of course pleased that

Étiemble praises Supervielle as the great poet who he was and who is too often underestimated; that he pays a rather warm tribute to Marcel Arland. But I cannot forget that what founds Rimbaud's originality completely escapes him, that *resonant voice* that seems to have come from elsewhere (perhaps because any idea of an 'elsewhere' was foreign to Étiemble). It seems more and more strange to me, and disappointing, even serious, that so many minds of a clearly superior quality so often err by unsound judgement, whereas their extensive knowledge, often the qualities of their heart, and the force of their intelligence should make them judge soundly. Note as well the illusions of so many left-wing intellectuals, first about the USSR, later about Mao; and note the case of Heidegger. (In regard to the latter, I have reread the notes taken in Germany, in 1935–36, by Denis de Rougemont. I have never thought that de Rougemont was a genius, nor even a great writer. But didn't he simply have enough *clear-sightedness*, enough *reason*, to understand immediately what was happening there, and what threat Hitler represented for us all? I remember watching the news, when I was a teenager, and seeing Hitler giving angry speeches, as well as a few Nazi demonstrations. How could any intellectual not see, not have seen, what these spectacles signified? Wasn't it—if ever there was a case for using the word—*glaring?*)

I would say as much about more recent images that we have all been able to see: the meetings on Tiananmen Square, the obligatory group readings of the *Little Red Book* even in the most remote regions of China. Today, can one look on without a sentiment of recoil, of fright, at the very least of great suspicion, at demonstrations where every individual is transformed into a mechanical doll, into a part of an immense, albeit merrily coloured, clock? *Why is one so blind?* (Indeed, Michel Leiris in China, for example.)

As for associating Hölderlin with Nazism, that's another famous absurdity.

*

There is perhaps a 'return to Goethe' (which will last, or not). My compatriot Adolf Muschg's short book, Handke's numerous references to his *oeuvre*, the new edition, at Gallimard, of *Conversations with Eckermann*, here and there the interest shown for his *Treatise on Colours*. As if one were clinging to what is most stable and full, after having idolized the geniuses of excess, anxiety or refusal: Hölderlin, Kleist, Nietzsche or that fragile angel who Novalis will have been. Like a last effort to wager on the yes addressed to the world, on the brink of a disaster whose signs are worsening and increasing. Perhaps a time has also come when one is weary of ghosts, demons, even angels, when the idea of a utopia is reformulated modestly; and when the

French word 'harmonie' evokes not only a brass band in a village.

(2 March)

The Ponge–Paulhan Correspondence. Isn't Paulhan's extraordinary ascendancy—like that of Gide before him—over several writers rather strange? In a man as apparently resolute and self-confident as Ponge, one would almost think of an amorous passion, with its fits of jealousy and absurd quarrels. In the end, will I not have been freer than many writers, with my art of fleeing, remaining silent, being absent? I don't think that criticism coming from Paulhan would have annihilated me, or that his few praises would have turned my head.

(15 March)

At almost eighty-five, Jean Tardieu reads a few of his texts with his old partner-in-crime, Lonsdale, at the Maison des Écrivains. He is enjoying himself as much as forty years ago, when he read Professor Froeppel's statements to us at his home, on the boulevard Arago. By listening to him, one can better evaluate a very French quality of his *oeuvre*: deep seriousness hidden beneath joking. I notice Claude Mauriac in the room, which is very small and full of friends.

The Seine is mud-coloured, as in my poem included in *The Barn-Owl* and also dated in the month of March—more than forty years ago.

(28 March)

The announcement of Giacinto Scelsi's death brings back the almost vanished memory of our several encounters in Rome, in 1946: he who was so afraid of mines, on the Fregene Beach, had his first stroke on a beach the other day. He was eighty-four years old and very close to Michaux. At the age of twenty-one, I had no idea that he would become an important composer in our century.

(10 August)

I have reread Malherbe's 'Saint Peter's Tears' because of the surprising analysis ventured by Ponge in his big book devoted to this poet whom he admires more than any other.

Christ's eyes looking at the renegade: 'Those beautiful sovereign eyes that cross the earth . . .'

The praise of the first martyrs, of the young death that will later move Rilke in, of course, a completely different way:

'O desirable end of their past pains!
Their feet, which have never trampled debris,
Make a superb floor of stars . . .'

And like Rilke later on, Malherbe pays tribute to their
mothers:

> 'And you, women three times, four times blest,
> Of these young loves the loving mothers,
> What are you doing for them, if you miss them?'

Another passage which, this time, more sensibly, reminds
me of Góngora (in his sonnet on Phaeton?):

> '. . . when his lowered eyes
> See the places where the trampled ground
> Has written vestiges of the Saviour's feet . . .'

The verses about the Dawn are admirable—and per-
haps praised somewhere by Larbaud?—with this theme
of a veil so present in Goethe's 'Zueignung':

> 'And of a veil woven of steam and storms . . .'

(5 December)

1989

The Goldberg Variations (in Gould's interpretation). I can only stutter about it. It is almost impossible to find intuitive analogies that would explain to you, at least in part, why it is so beautiful and sovereign; as opposed to what I have ventured about Purcell and Schubert. All the same, I noted this, without thinking further: a very strong sensation of *plenitude*; no tension towards something else, no 'Sehnsucht' but, rather, an equilibrium and an order. One cannot speak of 'heart', of sentiment, of passion; nor of a mystical élan. Perhaps: as if reason were jubilant? A force delighted to blossom, a mathematics that is jubilant— and conquering?

One surely does not think whatsoever of nature, of landscapes; at most, of constellations, yet constellations that would be visible in broad daylight, not at all against a black background, against an abyss as a backdrop. No reference either to what is human— faces or bodies; nor any reference to angels or gods.

Also this: the fast movements do not evoke dances; nor anything *burning*. An explosion of limpid figures, a very free and sovereign way of playing with time, a supreme lightness—yet, once again, neither elves nor angels—winged reason, and even then . . .

Or it would be as if all sorts of diverse élans, of rather conquering impulses found themselves decanted to the maximum without ceasing to be alive.

But the slow variations: this is where words are lacking. Hesitating, let me venture that they resemble what one could hear after crossing the Lethe in Dante's *Paradise*: words, inflexions that the human ear could grasp only on the highest storey of the world.

(2 March)

Ungaretti–Paulhan. On the TV yesterday, a rerun of the show *Lectures pour tous*, where Dumayet had invited Paulhan and Ungaretti. (First observation: *Lectures pour tous* was much more worthwhile than *Apostrophes*.) Paulhan was enjoying himself with great subtlety. Was he completely right in regard to 'informal' art and Fautrier? I am not entirely sure. But how intensely present Ungaretti was—it was perhaps the last year that I saw him in Paris—and what a capacity for passion that old man had, with his faun-like face!

Their correspondence has arrived this morning.

Well, I am disappointed by it, when I think of the quality of those two men and of the close friendship that bound them from beginning to end. Too much space is taken up by 'the literary life', that is, by the most visible *surface* of their two destinies (this evil is even more serious in the Paulhan–Saint-John Perse correspondence). I conclude from this, having so much loved and admired in Ungaretti his warmth, vehemence and generosity, that he is one of those writers of whom nothing, or almost, of what is essential goes into their letters.

But something else has now also struck me: that in Rilke's numerous letters that I have read, and sometimes translated, he never evokes the literary world, nor the success or lack of success of his books. And that this poet, who has been considered excessively narcissistic, appears most of the time as extremely attentive to his correspondents, almost always generous to them with his time and with his experience.

(30 October)

1990

Reading Saba, his poems from 1935–43, *Last Things*. As when reading Skácel, I felt a sort of vexation, if not shame, at having never been able to attain this supreme and, in fact, only apparent simplicity, linked, in both poets, to a long experience of suffering. One perhaps the price of the other. (However, maybe I am inventing this link.) From another collection 'Fruits and Vegetables':

> 'Grass, fruit, colours of the beautiful
> season. A few baskets in which sweet
> soft pulp is revealed to thirst.
> In comes a child, bare legs,
> headstrong, he runs off.
> > The humble
> shop darkens, gets old
> like a mother.
> > Outside, in the sunlight,
> he vanishes, with his weightless shadow.'

(28 March)

Keats, 'Ode to a Nightingale'.

When I read, unhappy that I have only rudiments of English, 'thou, light-winged Dryad of the trees', for example, I believe I am touching a pure marvel of poetry; and, deciphering the strophe not without difficulty, I wonder if the floral opulence of the summer has ever been better said. Since the short selection of the 'Orphée' series does not include this poem, I find only Pierre-Louis Matthey's version in French, a translation whose ending I criticized in *Une transaction secrète* (A Secret Transaction).

It is strange that the wild and ingenious adolescent Matthey brought to fame by *Seize à vingt* fell, later, into the decadent over-ornateness that can be found as well in the Cocteau of *Le Requiem* (The Requiem) or, differently, in an Olivier Larronde.

(6 April)

Marseilles. Poor little cousin Odile F., bald like a deported person, unrecognizable, despite her smile—but is it already somewhat mechanical?—her beautiful blue eyes, the big ring worn on one of her swollen fingers. Outside, the arid hills, the white limestone and, with no transition, above, the apartment buildings in the shape of towers or long rectangles.

Where is Celan's 'Singbarer Rest', his 'Singable remnant'?

(14 June)

Have just read Walser's *The Tanners*. Walser belongs to the family of Dhôtel, but his is a more singular child, and much more lost.

Also read Thomas's *Le Goût de l'éternel* (The Taste of the Eternal). It is an admirable book every time that he enters the burning zones of pain, desire and distress. The shadow of the death of his wife Jacqueline, Pierre Herbart's end, so true in its blend of derision and liberty. The total incomprehension in regard to such a book—but this has almost become the rule—of the so self-confident people of *Panorama*.

*

Issa. To the note in the *Second Seedtime*, page 143, let me add this:

> *Go outside for a breath of fresh air*
> *Was his advice, and I saw*
> *The moon's billhook above the gate.*

(19 June)

Calderón. How admirable is *The Constant Prince*, a play written in verse, in strict forms adapted to the tone of each moment (even the sonnets, which one would dream of translating). A striking proximity with Góngora, or so it seems to me, a layman. Because of the themes: the violence of faith and the sentiment of horror, which we will probably soon no longer understand at all.

(23 June)

Bashō. Rereading *The Narrow Road to the Deep North*, which I love so much, I once again come across iris leaves compared to swords, and the ritual that stems from this: covering roofs with such leaves, at such-and-such a date of the year, wards off demons. No later than yesterday in the garden, while looking at irises that had shed their flowers, I had indeed thought of swords—and almost immediately thereafter, of what, to my eyes, was irrelevant about this comparison. These echoes between ways of looking, feeling and speaking that are separated by almost exactly three centuries.

(26 June)

Noticed, towards six in the evening, the lit lamp of a house and, above it, the flamboyant purple clouds: the tame lamp of the bounding tiger?

(5 October)

Have received relatively few letters about *Notebook of Greenery*. The absence of some echoes suffices to make me have doubts about the warmth of others. In the end: one would like to be borne along in a palanquin of praise.

(29 October)

Cuba. A TV-documentary report in Havana. I think I understand the Latin American baroque style while looking at so many contrasts and mixtures: those old palaces in ruins and those carnivals with as bad a taste as the worst TV shows, the square where the rhumba is danced, the eighty-seven-year-old Black singer scratching his guitar, all those women who, from the little girl to the old lady, wriggle their hips lasciviously; or the old woman, like the survivor of a luxurious past, in her flat with extravagant furniture, beneath her portrait as a young poetess among her dogs. Then Miami with its outcast refugees, expressionist painters, a homosexual novelist who claims to feed himself exclusively with baby food because that corresponds, according to him, to his infantile side. (He committed suicide shortly thereafter.) The rain floods the courtyard of a dilapidated palace where a child and a dog are still playing.

(1 December)

Dream. Our friends the R.'s, from Vevey, are hosting a party in a vast hotel with a terrace: many guests here and there, as if circumstances that were similar in reality had been magnified—such as dreams often do. The terrace looks out on the no-less-great gardens of a seminary or convent. There, a sort of procession—about which I cannot say much, except that it was made up uniquely of women—is leading a young woman to her grave, unless it is to the spot where she will be executed. A 'sinner', probably. When this scene has occurred several times, and when at the end I see the victim closer up, who is almost a child, with black eyes, and Spanish-looking, such anger grips me that I intervene from the terrace with extremely violent words. Just as soon, I feel the embarrassment and the reprobation of the guests; but I especially dread the reaction of our dear hosts; and, indeed, I see L. R. leave the hotel lobby and when, nearing her husband sitting in a large armchair, I speak to him, I have to listen to him telling me, in friendly yet cold tones, that time would be needed until everything between us became as it had been before.

Upon this, I see myself going down the staircase leading to the terrace of the convent garden, a genuine old park with ivy and trees with yellowing leaves, where there are lots of scattered groups made up of rather elderly people who look more modest than the guests on the terrace. I spot our friend L. ringing the bell at a glass door, probably to attempt to see the Mother Superior and take care of things. But everyone around me is murmuring. Their anger is more and more noticeable; with the first insults—an old lady at a low window calls me Satan—I understand that, if I don't flee immediately, I risk being lynched. As I go back up the staircase, I still try to explain that, if I cried out, it was out of respect for religion.

(15 December)

1991

Shestov: 'The leitmotiv of all of Chekov's last works is this: "You sense that human beings aren't hearing you very well, that you need to raise your voice, shout. But shouting disgusts you. So you begin speaking softer and softer, and soon you will be able to stop speaking entirely."'

Shestov once again, on constraint: 'It didn't cross its [Catholicism's] mind that what needs to be protected by the principle of contradiction, or by henchmen and jailors, lies beyond divine truth; and that what saves mankind is precisely that which is, according to human measures, weak, feeble-minded, and deprived of all protection.'

(11 January)

War, the show begins. May it be short, as one seems to hope this morning.

(17 January)

The worst can still be feared, and the outbursts of hatred nonetheless foreseeable. These abscesses, as formerly in the Balkans, that are left to fester too long.

Reading Goethe's *Iphigenia in Taurus* at the same time as this becomes especially difficult. Dostoevsky is better suited to times of crisis.

(18 January)

> War, hideous in all respects.
> War, which makes us drop our pens.

(21 January)

It's almost light out at six in the evening.

(22 January)

Kafka. His terrible last letters to his parents: the well-intentioned little boy who wants to reassure, not to complain, and lives in dark poverty—and whose few books dominate the century. The power of the insect.

(6 February)

After having seen the Seine swollen by the spring rains, on 14 March 1947, I had written a short poem that includes these words: 'The waters never the same / nor the days. He who would take water in his hands...' This came back to memory when I discovered, in Goethe's *Divan*, the poem, probably from 1816, in which he contrasts Greek plastic-arts taste to his new love of fluidity, represented by the act of diving voluptuously into the Euphrates, and which concludes with this quatrain:

> 'Löscht ich so der Seele Brand,
> Lied es wird erschallen;
> Schöpft des Dichters reine Hand,
> Wasser wird sich ballen.'

> [If I snuff out the fire of the soul,
> Song will ring out;
> If a pure-handed poet creates,
> Water will become a ball.]

This image came to Goethe from a beautiful Indian legend where a woman, as long as she keeps a pure heart, has the power of bringing back the river water in her hands, without the aid of any recipient; but once desire crosses her heart, the water flows between her fingers.

The calamity is not being able to render into French the perfection of the last two lines, which are almost proverb-like, on the magical power reserved to the pure.

(16 February)

A dry rose petal slipped into a letter from Canada: it has the exact colours of some winter sunsets, the yellow at the horizon, the pink higher up, both equally diaphanous.

(20 February)

In the Schiller–Goethe correspondence, I notice that Goethe did not attend the performance, in Weimar on 25 January 1796, of Mozart's *Don Giovanni*, whereas he went to several other evenings during the same festivities.

Also notable is that one of Schubert's friends, who sent to Goethe in 1817 or 1818 a selection of lieder based on the poet's texts, received no response.

(27 February)

This morning, 28 February, at six o'clock, the announcement of the end of the Gulf War.

(28 February)

Henri Thomas seriously ill. I am reading what risks being his last book, which he has announced to me as his 'last grimace', a very painful return to his childhood, with Rimbaud there to 'save' him. It is a short poignant book, *Do I Have a Country?*

(30 April)

Italy. Fragments from the night of 22–23 June:

> *It's the good [proud?] inn of the grass*
> *its unlaced breastplate*
> *it's whiter than the moon*

the horse off to the side neighs because it's not his
it's something hardly less strange than death

(22–23 June)

It's strange. Even now, I almost never think of the past. Every now and then, a dream is needed to bring it back. Such as the very recent dream, where a meal brought together members of my family, I no longer remember where nor why; a few of those many aunts and uncles whom I had and who are, of course, all dead. From this dream, I only recall that it was I who served at the table. When I awoke, I thought that this was because, in any case, I was nearing them.

Similarly, with my shoulder afflicted by an onset of arthritis, I told myself that it was like an arrow stuck in my back so that I would come closer to the wounded, so that I would at last have pain elsewhere than in my mind, and that it would teach me, if possible.

(28 November)

Schiller and Goethe. In 1799, Goethe is fifty years old and, in the eyes of posterity, this is the acme of their common glory. However, when they tried to launch a review, *Propylaea*, devoted to the arts, they have difficulty finding four hundred and fifty readers and keep deploring the mediocrity of the German public.

(10 December)

Apropos of Quignard's book *All the World's Mornings*, which is in fact very beautiful, of the publicity campaign that is promoting it because of Alain Corneau's film, which is not so good as that and is based on the novel, and of my recent visit to Henri Thomas: I tell myself that, in this affair, it is Quignard who is playing the role of Marin Marais and Thomas that of Sainte-Colombe. For Quignard, the visible success, the applause of the Court; for Thomas, the wooden cabin, the ordeal and the true melody of pain.

(16 December)

1993

Paid a visit to Jean Tortel, whom we hadn't seen for about a year, if not more. Jeannette is going to turn ninety years old and hardly seems to have changed since we have known her: when she was sixty, she had the same small, rather crumpled face and a not-very-graceful figure; but what vigour, what mental tranquillity, what presence! Jean, however, can no longer move unless she supports him. He wears sunglasses, can't hear very well and can't see much either; he can thus no longer read, nor write, which is equivalent, for a man like him, to barely exist. Although he suffers much because of this, he has kept for his wife and friends that affectionate warmth that has always moved us in his regard; all the more so, today, in that we no longer responded, as our hearts dictated us to do, the day, already long in the past, when he 'modernized' his poetry—but this is not putting it well—which earned him admiration as a model and caused him to be courted by people who, rightly or wrongly, are totally foreign to me! Not Henri Deluy or even Arseguel, who are both friendly, but Viton, Liliane Giraudon or Royet-Journoud. As a result, the poets who move me the most manifestly became strangers to Tortel: not only Bonnefoy and Thomas, but also

Paul de Roux and Jean-Pierre Lemaire; and that we could not agree on much more, I fear, than on Du Bouchet—who has kept all his admiration for Tortel.

With every visit, I thus had to keep to myself my true sentiments in this field, since an avowal would have created a too-great distance between us; and so attached as I still am to an entire part of his *oeuvre*, and not exclusively to the oldest part.

What remains is this admirably warm, clear-minded and intelligent man for whom poetry, his wife and his garden will seemingly have been all his life; so that, each time, this radiance made me pass over our differences and sense some remorse at not having met him more often.

With this, a surprising lack of sensibility for music and painting, and never, as far as I know, did he take trips. An extremely 'classic' limitation to the edges of his garden, extremely 'classic French' in fact.

The relationship of his *oeuvre*, of his short poems, with some of Rameau's compositions—even as they also prolong Tristan L'Hermite and other poets from that period, of which he has spoken so well. Mallarmé remains for him, evidently, the major reference.

(The period of the *Cahiers du Sud* will have been, to all appearances, the great adventure of their lives: I indeed believe, whereas we would always listen much more than we spoke, we will not have paid a single visit to them without hearing them go back to some of those episodes: even as other people evoke the First World War—there are fewer and fewer of them—or the years of the French Underground. Minor faults which make one smile more than they irritate but which confirm a certain narrowness of experience.—Too much 'literature'!)

(5 February)

On 14 March, Arseguel informs me by telephone of the death of Jean Tortel, who is going to be buried on the same day as, in Lausanne, our great friend Dr Lehmann.

(1 March)

A political dream. In an electoral campaign between the right and the left, the right, which has the majority, shows an arrogant confidence in its success; but a few signs, little by little, to our great relief, show that the left is not only rising again but that it is going, almost certainly, to win the election. It then appears subsequently that this is not a genuine election but, rather, a sort of question-and-answer game such as takes place on television, in which representatives of two opposing political parties compete.

As Mitterrand is sitting there in front of us in an armchair (perhaps one of those film-director's chairs with his name written on the back), I see my daughter, as a child, starting to shake the chair from the back; and this makes me indignant, a reaction which I convey to a lady next to me, and I tell her that young people today don't respect anything or anyone any more.

At this, Mitterrand, who is being interviewed, declares that he sees in front of him figures, or women, black women; this evidently means that he sees his end as near. However, almost as soon, these figures become visible for us as well: they are black hippopotamuses swimming in the water of a vast pond, such as many documentary films have shown us, and emerging more or less from the water; while a shadow, equally black, a silhouette—we don't know— quickly goes across the background. (It seems that the 'hippopotamus' had first appeared as a simple word in the question-and-answer game.)

I thought, still inside the dream perhaps or, more probably, afterwards, of Ungaretti's last poem, 'The Petrified and the Velvet', in which he evokes the reefs that await him in the sea.

(13 August)

Proust in *Jean Santeuil* apropos of Mme de Réveillon, who is the fictional mask here of Anna de Noailles: 'What made up the very nature of the poetry of this great poet (Mme Gaspard de Réveillon) never appeared in what she said, but, on the contrary, through her constant joking, through her scoffing at such-and-such a person who was speaking of spring, or love, and so on, for she would have seemed to look down on such things; and when one spoke to her about herself, she seemed to be a person loving only good cooking, laziness and the bed. It's not at all that her poems were not sincere, but, on the contrary, that they expressed something that in her was so profound that she had not even been able to think about it, speak about it, define it as something different than the self, and that she would have perhaps considered doing so as a kind of sacrilege. [. . .] But this intimate essence of things, of which she didn't speak, was in fact the only essence that was really important to her . . .'

(Advice, of sorts, to all those who, on the contrary, are inexhaustible about what is most secret part of themselves and of their *oeuvres*.)

(10 October)

Brief trip to Stockholm. When I arrived, a little lost, at the Esplanade Hotel, which has a rather pleasant modern (?) architecture, I had to clear a way, carrying my suitcase, through a group of photographers and scantily dressed models as remote and beautiful as they are taught to be: one would think I had landed among the houris promised in Muhammad's Paradise.

On the 5th, accompanied by my translator, Bengt Erasmie, a day once again marked by very grey weather—from my hotel room, I sometimes heard the sound of hooves on cobblestones: it was a carriage and team of horses driven by a very dignified coachman, wearing a black uniform and going back to the Royal Stables—and it seemed to me that I was beginning to make out in Stockholm, some of whose big avenues recalled Zurich, the 'beautiful' department stores as well as the architecture that was rather heavy and opulent-looking, as also were the passers-by; many blonde women with short smooth hair, with rose complexions exuding health, like merry, rather-too-decent women skiing champions; at the hotel, my breakfast had been served to me by a tall, thin young woman whose pale blonde hair was tied by a black ribbon and whose skirt went down all the way to her heels, as if she had walked right out of one of Larsson's paintings and 'good as gold', was keeping her eyes obstinately lowered.

After visiting, at the Vasa Museum, the beautiful reconstructed wrecked ship, which is impressive because of its size, the beauty of its sculptures and its black colour, we are going to take a small boat in the district of Luna Park, deserted at this hour: it is a rather desolate seashore. Erasmie shows me three boats, moored to the opposite quay, which are black and yellow and with a higher silhouette than the others: icebreakers, he tells me. This word will have almost more echo in me than any image of the city. We cross the water; the ticket collector is a young Asian woman, the few passengers are rather poorly dressed. Water is everywhere, the cold is biting; some quays are lined with rather beautiful, old, yellow or dull-ochre mansions; others, like the one to which we are heading, display rather sad-looking modern blocks of flats, garages and offices. (In the end, of the few days that I will have spent in Sweden, without even awakening the memory of my gloomy reading in front of ten-odd poor wretches, it's an impression of sadness that will especially stay with me.)

Once we had disembarked, a lift enabled us to go up to the top of a hill from which a little park offers a view that Strindberg apparently described in one of his novels (there are a few beautiful little landscapes painted by him at the National Museum). A little further, after entering the bar of a small theatre to get warm, we are jovially welcomed in French by a big woman with almost Fellini-like hair, amid young ear-ringed rock-music fans who are surprised but by no means aggressive; on the podium of a neighbouring room, a girl is practicing a tap-dancing act.

The old district is beautiful, but a little dismal: a few antique shops, a closed church, only a few pedestrians.

The next day, a holiday still as grey and dark, grey and *dull*, as the preceding days. A few very beautiful paintings at the National Museum: two perfect little Cranachs, very beautiful portraits by Rembrandt and the strange unfinished composition, reddish and blond-coloured, of the 'Conspiracy of the Batavians', the 'Simeon's Song of Praise' that would be one of his last works.

(14 November)

Audiberti's letters to Paulhan: one would say a child writing to the man on whom depends the essential of his existence; rich, inventive letters that show the extent of Paulhan's generosity in their friendship, even if his letters have been lost. It is a book that arouses, if this were necessary, sympathy for both correspondents. But what about Audiberti's poetry? Paulhan was severe about Audiberti's novels, spoke little about his plays, but showed much warmth to the poetry. What remains of it today? Audiberti was himself the first to nurture doubts about this activity *per se*.

I am leafing again through *Toujours* (Always), bought in 1945, while I was still in Lausanne (and inside the book I find a page of my father's tear-off 'Veterinaria A. G. Zurich' calendar for 1943). Some poems are pencil-marked with a cross. What turns me away from them is their Hugolian scale as well as their frequent hermetic quality. But sometimes a verbal genius is deployed, with a great singularity of tone, which still amazes me ('Au soldat noyé', 'To the Drowned Soldier'). The best part of his poetry perhaps lies in his short verse, the vigorous song, at once vulgar and metaphysical.

(23 November)

1994

This morning the air of the streets had a few minute snowflakes, like gnats made of snow.

(24 January)

The pianist Christian Zacharias spoke admirably of Schumann last night on Arte. Especially evoking that 'ferne Stimme', that 'voice come from afar' in a piece whose name I have forgotten, voice that he imagines as a motif of the *Saint John Passion*—the 'Es ist vollbracht' ('It is accomplished')—that he also thinks he notices in one of Suzanne's arias in *The Marriage of Figaro* and in the slow movement of Beethoven's Opus 110: all exceedingly beautiful and moving examples.

(A precision about the motif of the 'ferne Stimme': it's in the 8th Novelette and apparently borrowed from Clara Wieck; as to the Adagio of Opus 110, it is the 'Klagender Gesang', or 'Tearful Song'. It matters little to me whether he is right or wrong, since the value of what he compares is so high.)

(3 February)

In a multichannel package of documentary films offered by the TV as a tribute to Juliette Gréco, I see once again, not without surprise, someone of whom no one speaks, Gabriel Pomerand—and not without a little emotion (all the more so in that I had come across him in the *Journal* of Lélo Fiaux, whom he entranced for a few days and who calls him 'Pomerand-me-I-Gabriel-the-archangel'). His bony Kalmyk face, his nervous leaps on the Passerelle des Arts, his burps while declaiming a Lettrist poem. We were not made to get along together, but I remember that his vulnerability sometimes moved me, and that he had a heart. He was someone who made a little noise in Saint-German-des-Prés for a while (a few months?), who more or less sincerely believed that he was a new Rimbaud—and who has completely vanished from the horizon.

(7 February)

The very pale sun through the clouds suddenly makes me recall the object that I loved, when I was a child, at my aunt L.'s, in Moudon: a parchment screen behind which a candle could be burned.

(11 February)

The Adagio of Beethoven's string quartet Opus 59, No. 2, that monument—as probably likewise are other slow movements of the string quartets—making one think of mountains, such as I begin to rediscover them in my memory, or such as I saw them during a recent trip to Switzerland, beyond Lake Neuchâtel, with Mont Blanc royal and remote: very high lines crisscrossing, slopes with different textures, bright fragments of ice.

(11 March)

With its budding leaves, the fig tree is, in the morning, a one-hundred-branch candelabrum—lit up.

(24 March)

A few verses by Mashrab, 'the flamboyant vagabond', the 'extravagant pilgrim', and a half-mythical figure of the eighteenth century, originally from what is currently the country of Uzbekistan:

> 'Arriving in Andijan where his mother was living, he thought: "Mashrab, since your departure, eighteen years have gone by, first see is your mother is still alive . . ."
>
> He slowly neared his mother's door, looked into the courtyard.
>
> Slowly I go in the morning, slowly, onto her threshold
> Slowly, I rub, slowly, the dust of her door from my eyes.'

Elsewhere:

> 'Even if I am a sinner, I am not in despair
>   because of the door:
> For a single rose, water must be given to one
>   hundred thousand thorns . . .'

Finally, in his poem about the pilgrim, about he who passes by:

> 'Don't ask me who I am, me, Mashrab the
>   vagabond!
> Wherever man is burning, I water his fire
>   with my tears and keep going.'

(29 March)

To my quotations from Plato's *Republic*, in *The Second Seedtime*, page 222, add this observation:

In the myth of Er, the souls choose the form of their new existence. Ulysses' soul finds itself being the last one to choose: it opts for a life away from others, an obscure existence—declaring that it would not have made another choice if it had been first on the list.

(25 April)

Pleasant evening at Truinas, yesterday, the 9th. The rosebushes in the very high grass, the stones from which the walls of the terraces are made, and the harder, more severe stones of the house.

The friendship of someone like André du Bouchet fortifies, because of his unshakable faithfulness to what is essential. I am not surprised that he has been, after me, deeply affected by Hölderlin's admirable fragment, 'Columbus':

'since
for so little
the bell used
for ringing out
dinnertime
was out of tune, as if by the snow.'

(10 July)

Awakened at dawn: the mauve-coloured mountain, the gilded dust of the first sunrays, the cool air, the silvery sky on the horizon. Alb: I am thinking of the priest's vestment that bears this name. Could one bow down like that priest who is absent and, perhaps, less necessary now?

I am also thinking of Mallarmé's short poem involving a bracelet for, probably, what is marvellously feminine about dawn. In fact, the poem speaks about an evening twilight but it is no less admirable:

'The sceptre of rosy shores
Stagnant on eves of gold, this is it,
This closed white flight you place
Against the fire of a bracelet.'

(12 August)

Since our trip to Italy, from 18 to 24 September, with
our friends the R's, was less successful than so many
other trips (because of too much haste, and especially
because of the feeling, which we too often had, that
we were having a little trouble making our respective
admirations contagious; probably also because, simply
stated, our friends are getting older, and mixed in with
all this is the way habits wear one down), I wish to
retain from my notes the little that is worthwhile:

At the Grand-Saint-Bernard tunnel, the whole
country grey under the snow and, once the border had
been crossed: sunlight, a few spotless, bright white
summits. Farther down, in the Aosta Valley, it seems
that someone has become aware of the beauty of old
vine arbours mixed with boulders and has begun
'showing them to their advantage', so that, like many
other things today, they have become less surprising
and less 'genuine'.

The colours of Monferrat are rather dark, deep
shades of yellow, ochre and green, beneath the alps of

clouds—which will become simple sails on the sea, glimpsed on the open sea in front of Genoa.

In the olive groves of the Ligurian Riviera, large rust-coloured nets are rolled up from tree to tree or spread out at their bases for future harvestings.

In Florence, the moving surprise of seeing the Duomo again at the end of a street, while walking by; we won't have the time to go in.

Meal at the Giostra Club, a small restaurant, especially favoured by Italians despite its absurd name, which consists of a narrow corridor kept a little too cool by means of big fans. The owner wears a kind of soft chef's hat that seems to have come directly from one of Ghirlandaio's frescos, which his facial features would not detract from, either; the boy and girl who are serving, the latter very pretty and with bare arms, are perhaps his children. Because Michel R. has ordered the most expensive wine, the owner ceremoniously decants it into a carafe and has it tasted in a way worthy of a magician (he will repeat only an abbreviated form the next day, because of the cheaper price of the wine chosen that evening).

[. . .]

Leaving there for Bologna, we make a stop at Grizzana, to pay tribute to Morandi. It is hardly more than a few ordinary houses grouped around a crossroads. The grocery at which we buy some bars of soap has an uncle who used to fetch Morandi at the station—the Vergato station, probably. In vain, we seek out the artist's house, in front of which we must have walked without doubting that it was such an ordinary abode. But the moving landscape reminds me of that of the Drôme, yet it is more arid here, and the architecture of the houses is simpler, without charm or ornamentation.

Welcome surprise of an exhibition at the town hall, barely guarded in fact, titled *Clouds of Absence*. Reading the catalogue informs me that the violence of the war, in 1943–1944, did not spare this valley: allied bombings of the viaducts and the roads, underground movement acts, Nazi repression in Grizzana itself. Morandi, afflicted and remaining silent when facing these tragedies.

[. . .]

Bologna: overcast skies. Long visit to the Morandi Museum, ever with the same emotion of astonishment in front of the last canvases, already seen in Marseilles.

[. . .]

Parma: a town surprisingly calm and airy, after Florence and Bologna. The Baptistery has been cleaned too much, but the interior, which recalls Ravenna, remains admirable. It is difficult to admire, without forcing oneself to do so, Correggio's cupola, which is too distant and too virtuoso. There are few tourists. In the evening, after an exquisite meal at Parizzi's, we go back to the piazza Duomo, hardly lit. An amorous couple; two boys sitting on the pavement and smoking; a young woman who is sitting on the marble bench of the baptistery and is perhaps a drug addict or a deserted wife, or simply romantic. I am invaded by an increasing, very moving sentiment of calmness, of somnolence, even of dreaminess.

On Friday morning, the countryside in the fog, the mist over the rifle range with its four coloured targets; the towering tree and the peacock in the park of the Magnani-Rocca Foundation—the Cézannes and the Morandis that Mme Pizzetti generously got out for us, placing them on a big table.

[. . .]

Parma: I would willingly reread Bertolluci's *Camera da letto* (The Bedroom), slowly, to walk once again in these streets with other eyes.

Apropos of Morandi, perhaps it is not necessary to add much to my lines in *Autres journées* (Other Days). But it is certain that looking once again at a large selection confirms his greatness and his magnificent isolation in our century. Do not forget his bedside reading: Pascal and Leopardi.

(3–5 October)

Dream. Fragments of a long, extravagant dream, per-
haps linked to the affair of the Temple Solaire sect
which is being much talked about. It seems to me
that everything was revolving around a case full of
wine bottles one of which apparently contains, or
hides, a mysterious and probably very dangerous
substance. [While recopying this note today, in 2009,
I remember an excellent film, by Hitchcock probably,
where this motif is central: *The Thirty-Nine Steps*?]
Someone, thus, is devoting himself to this cover-
up job inside a more or less empty, high-ceilinged
building—a kind of high barn with two storeys—and
stashing away 'the thing' in a hole of one of the very
high walls; then building a whole scaffolding to con-
ceal and, if necessary, defend the hiding place.

Then, probably after other episodes, someone was
having me—I who was in another building close to
the other one—smell something: was it a dish of food,
or a drink with an orange-blossom fragrance?—while
I was beginning to sense, coming from the building
with the hiding place, another smell, like jam begin-
ning to burn, to cram: an odour that betrayed the
'thing' so carefully concealed there. A very bizarre
story; and it seems to me that the character responsible
for the building with the hiding place was a sort of
Shylock and that all the dream had a colourful atmo-
sphere of an Italian Renaissance chronicle.

(10 October)

Bonnefoy. Apropos of Poussin, I am rereading *Rome, 1630*. From his extremely solid knowledge of the painting and the art of that period, he draws interpretations which indeed form a deep perspective but which are perhaps too personal to be always totally convincing. But I am in a bad position to judge; and, anyway, one never reads him without benefits.

An example: Is what he sees in Bernini's Baldachin in Saint Peter's Basilica really founded? Often, I believe that his personal dream, which is deep and admirable, impregnates his eyes too much; that he believes and wants to believe what matters so passionately to him to believe. Whatever might be the case with this, it moves me.

(31 October)

The State of Things by Wim Wenders: a strange, intelligent film that begins with the shooting of a science-fiction film that begins by evoking an imminent catastrophe and continues, when the shoot is forced to be interrupted, with a period when the crew waits in a deserted hotel of Sintra, only to end in a police film in Los Angeles—with a very beautiful moment where, in a trailer probably rolling towards death—as can be surmised, and this will be the case—and at the same time towards dawn, a counterpoint is at stake between the film director who is meditating on death and the end of all human history, and the mafia-linked producer who incessantly hums a song with a Hollywood (?) theme. To be truthful, a grim film: one leaves the initial fictive nightmare only to see denounced, in the forced pause of the shoot, the emptiness and the solitude of each of the crew; the cameraman, played by old Samuel Fuller, is waiting for the announcement of his wife's death, news that doesn't take long in getting to him and bringing him back to Los Angeles; an actress practices playing the violin, clumsily, and confides her anxiety to a shrink called in to save her; another actress avows to the man with whom she has just slept her weariness with what appears 'always the same story'; everyone drinks too much; and the hotel itself is almost a concrete ruin beaten by the waves of an enraged ocean . . .

The whole of this in black and white, like the announcement of a death.

Once more, after leaving this beautiful film, I told myself that the 'death of God' doesn't necessarily lead to a party but to emptiness; when thinking again of Antonioni's *Red Desert*, of *La Dolce vita* and many other contemporary films that are genuinely funereal.

(This is not the case, to go back to my current reflections, with Morandi's art, despite what Bonnefoy seems to say.)

(16 November)

Reread my notes on Morandi with relative satisfaction. They are things painted in the intimate room, in the 'room of the heart'—as this is not the case of almost any other modern *oeuvre*; at home, as near the centre as possible, whence the quiet radiance of the paintings and their frail majesty.

To acknowledge this fortifies my oldest convictions.

(25 November)

[To the pages of *The Second Seedtime* where I cite Joubert, I would willingly add today (2009) these, which I left out of that book back then. Thus:]

Joubert is a lover of water, of all forms of water. Having translated Hesiod at the age of nineteen, he quotes the verses that call for respecting the purity of fountains and rivers. During those same years, he marvellously describes the effects of rain ('While it is raining, there is kind of darkness that makes all objects seem longer . . .') which call for communion. After which: 'What makes waters consoling is their movement and their limpidity . . .' Thus, a thread of sensibility can weave, across time, links that are as close as they are marvellous. The same applies to his notes on twilight: 'How everything unperceptively grows silent at nightfall. How everything then seems to commune . . .' This is not far either from that Morandi about whom I have often mused recently.

Elsewhere: 'Shadow of God you who make us gleam . . .'

'Clarity alone should suffice for making happy.'

(1–5 December)

In *Ego scriptor*, a selection of Valéry's notebooks. He had spoken of the early morning, and concludes his note thus: 'God is not implausible, at this hour. The memory of a creation is not very far away. The Fiat lux is a very simple thing that has been seen and heard.'

Elsewhere: 'Dawn. It is not dawn—but the waning of the moon, gnawed pearl, melting ice—a dying glimmer replaced little by little by the new-born day. I love this moment, so pure, final, initial.'

And this, on the same page: 'Nothing moves me more than the morning in summer.'

The best Valéry is this one, almost still spontaneous and liking so much to get up early.

(15 December)

In George Steiner's book on Heidegger, this: 'It is hidden Being that gives the rock its dense "thereness", that makes the heart pause when a kingfisher alights, that makes our own existence inseparable from that of others. In each case, wonder and reflection tell us of an intensity of presentness . . .'

I do not know if he is quoting, or paraphrasing, one of Heidegger's texts, or if he himself introduces the example of the bird; but it is an exact translation of my fundamental poetic experience. Truth is the 'non-concealed', the 'un-veiled' (according to the Greek etymology).

(29 December)

1995

The water of the sky, in the evening. The coupe of
water. In the cold season.
The mother-of-pearl of the fast-fallen evening. The
cold sunlight on the stones.

(2 January)

One generally forgets, because of the old imagery of
the 'flames of Hell' that float somewhere in our mind,
that the depths of Hell, for Dante, are 'a lake of ice
stretching beneath my feet, / more like a sheet of
glass than frozen water . . .', a place of the greatest
constriction and hardness, where skulls and teeth bang
against each other like stones—the very thing that
would come back up to the surface of the real world,
more than six centuries later, in the camps of Kolyma.
Leafing through, today, the too-vague notes I happen
to have taken about this work, I suddenly realize that,
at the very end of this terrible first stage of their jour-
ney, it is thanks to the noise of a stream that Dante and
Virgil find the way out:

'Below somewhere there is a space, as far
from Beelzebub as the limit of his tomb,
known not by sight but only by the sound

of a little stream that makes its way down here
through the hollow of a rock that it has worn,
gently winding in gradual descent.

My guide and I entered that hidden road
to make our way back up to the bright world . . .'

There is nothing surprising about this. More than once
during an infinitely easier, more anodyne journey, I
will have had the same guide to get me disentangled.

*

The winter-coloured magpie, squawking as can the
voice of old age.

(6 January)

A big planet in the bare lime-tree branches and low
on the horizon, at the end of night. And since there is
hoarfrost, the grass crackles under my feet; I don't
know why this noise and this sensation have some-
thing pleasant about them; it must be linked to the idea
of coolness; or to that of a kind of breaking that would
not be painful, on the contrary; somewhat as when one
breaks bread? Or would that kind of happiness be
attached to the memory, however purely bookish yet
no less intense for that, of ice breaking up in rivers?
Would one then even feel the sandals of Spring on
one's feet?

(19 January)

In the end: I find only at night, in my nightmares, the worst, the most implacable part of reality, that with which the news swamps us day after day until we feel sick; and the real life that I lead, that infinitely privileged life, would begin to look rather like a dream, in the 'rosy' sense of the term.

(20 January)

Almost transparent smoke rising from fires in February; and further on, hardly higher, hovering in the very pale blue of the sky, those white clouds that we could all but believe are snowy Alpine mountains.

*

A strange scene of which I am unsure whether I dreamt it, or made it up between wakefulness and sleep, a sort of apologue: two chess players whose chessboard is floating on the water of a small stream, slack at that spot, in the silvery shadow of a big walnut tree; one player is knitting his brows during the effort he is making to win the match while the other has an absent look as if he already knows that the chessboard, sooner or later, will sink into the water, despite the laws of physics, with all its ivory chessmen.

(2 March)

Mountains of Savoy, seen beyond Lake Geneva: their full gown, their dark drape (black spotted with ermine); their true majesty.

One evening, other Alps, much farther, beyond another lake, suddenly take on the colour of an orchard of peach trees in blossom; they don't weigh much more.

(27 March)

Dream fragments. In the first one, I am told or I notice that Lionel Jospin is using a letter by Baudelaire to his mother for the purposes of electioneering advertising; I don't know whether it is in the form of tracts, or by mobilizing the pages of newspapers, and this doesn't matter much. Simply, in this dream, I think that this is very beautiful of him yet suicidal: governing a state having only little to do with poetry.

Then, I find myself in the old kitchen, with its shiny beige-painted walls, of the last flat in which my parents lived together, and I see it very realistically as it was back then; even the dilapidated shutters that are half-closed and that I struggle to open completely onto the garden while musing that we should get the owners to replace them, all the same. There is disorder on the tables, vegetable peelings—especially of leeks—and even a little dense, brown garden soil: it could be that my mother, although it is nearly noon and this is by no means habitual for her, is still sleeping, since she and my father had come home particularly late the night before. I thus wish to tidy up things a little while waiting for her to get up; but, above all, I look for a glass in which to place a small bouquet of snowdrops that I have just picked and that are so fragile that, if I don't hurry, they will soon wither. In fact, when the glass is finally found and I want to arrange them in it, the flowers have already fallen. I then hear my mother and my sister speaking in the next room.

After this episode, I still remember a brief exchange of words between two other people, probably two old servants, a man and a woman, and the strange turn of phrase that one of them uses: 'A star case'—and at the same time, through the window, the dark trees of the garden can be seen—a turn of phrase that they interpret, unless it is I who do so, ever inside the dream, in this way: 'It means being rather stooped and never doing anything but obey'; upon which I notice, strangely, that, indeed, 'a star case' can mean only that.

Since I then wake up—it is still night—I wonder if the verse by Baudelaire, 'The great-hearted servant of whom you were so jealous', which opens one of his most beautiful poems, indeed one of the most beautiful poems in the French language, to my tastes, might perhaps have been the main thread of all these images, since the mother, the flowers, the servant woman and death come together in it; and another fragment of a poem comes back to memory, more vaguely, to the extent that I first attribute it to Pierre Delisle, whereas I will find it the next day among Jean Tardieu's poetry (why has he also left us, why is he depriving us of his childlike, mischievous smile, when we were vaguely counting on him, once and for all?); and there too, in one of his most beautiful poems in a solemn style: 'Old, old stars, white hair dust / women of the dawn's poor housework / since I'm the one telling you I'll protect you / we'll get old together . . .'

Sooner or later, no bouquet will be able to be saved, no table tidied up. However, at this night's end, which will result in such a bright day, a sky invaded, for the first time in years, by a genuine crowd of swifts seemingly whirling at the end of an invisible rope held by an invisible and frenzied player, the absolute strangeness of Being catches hold of me: these thousands of years during which we will have been nothing and those other probable thousands of years in which we will be nothing, if not, for still a little time, an image or a word preserved in the dream of another person; and between these two emptinesses, the possibility to be traversed, in a dream, by these reflections of things or dead human beings and these merely imagined elements, only then to open one's eyes again and find the 'true' flowers—which will not be snowdrops, but periwinkles perhaps, or gillyflowers, because it is already summer—and be able to fetch a 'true' glass in which to arrange them before they wither, but not to be able to wake up your mother, who, in fact, in her whole life, will probably never have once slept until noon. . . Vertigo has quickly seized you in front of these encounters between such different states of the 'reality' in which we are immersed and of which one no longer knows at all what it might be.

(30 April)

The word 'élucubration' (wild imaginings): 'staying up late, labour that a piece of work has demanded; a piece of work made up of work and late nights'; the word often understood as a synonym of thoughts more or less laboriously extravagant. The word could be useful to me as the title for a gathering of texts, with this note: '*Élucubrations*: work accomplished by lamplight, often understood as laborious, if not extravagant; whatever the case, accomplished during nocturnal hours, in darkness or against darkness; in the latter case, before they are definitively victorious, without our being able to measure what advance we still keep over them.'

(8 May)

The fragrance of iris, very sweet, sugary, almost suave, evoking, it seems to me, the idea that an adolescent can have of the feminine: what makes you turn your head . . . With that kind of bright yellow, solar, caterpillar, but so well hidden under pale blue petals as if beneath tongues of water. But the word 'caterpillar' is disturbing, and 'brush' just as much. A reserve of gold powder, a fur of gold, a golden fleece perhaps, hidden under the silk of the robe?

(10 May)

1996

Friedhelm Kemp has sent me several documents concerning Christine Lavant, including a photograph where a black veil framing her face gives her the look of a Mother Superior. A body that one makes out as frail, a big knotty peasant's hand and a big face with deeply marked, beautiful, noble features; very big eyes, a prominent nose, a finely delineated mouth. Indeed, she is like a nun in a Renaissance painting. When she was photographed (when she won the Trakl Prize), she was forty-nine years old.

(15 March)

This note by Meschonnic to his translation of the Book of Wisdom (The Ecclesiast): '*Orchards*, this is the word for *paradise* in Persian: etymologically, the enclosure. The orchard is also paradisiac in Celtic mythology: Avallon.' This shows that one can innocently, unconsciously, recover the oldest dreams of mankind.

(28 November)

Last Saturday, the burial of poor L. C. It seemed to me that it was also that of the Catholic Church itself.

A Mass dispatched in a half-hour by a priest who was a friend of the family, who had baptised the child and who cared more about telling his assistants where to stand and to explain why he was sprinkling holy water on the casket than to speak to the grief-stricken parents. Without a word for the brutality of the tragedy (did he fear that it was a suicide?—it is not known what exactly happened to those two unfortunate young people), hardly a word about L. himself; as if in haste, the priest skipped over to the outcome of the tragedy, to this boy who, 'seeing God'—and he didn't dwell on that either, very much. Death thus becomes a simple administrative formality, aggravated even more by ridiculous hymns and the total absence of any other music. And that altar boy in a pullover, our own 'village idiot', in fact such a touching figure, holding the bucket of holy water with his mouth gaping open or swinging the censer with so much energetic enthusiasm that one saw the moment when it would crash against the chapel wall . . .

I couldn't keep myself from thinking then of that burial of Marie-Louise Bourdon, which I evoked in *Seedtime*, where the beauty of the liturgical words gave the impression of blessing the departure of a boat on a river flowing towards the Beyond.

(9 December)

1997

The much-desired rain having returned: but we will soon tire of it.

Fatigue. The misfortune of friends evokes the high tide when it is seen rising around a boulder on which one can barely linger. This makes your heart bleed. What is ineluctable—from which a shorter and shorter distance or a thinner or thinner protection shelters us.

The other evening, I had the impression of reading, for the first time, on the furrowed face of our friend W. the four letters of the word 'mort' (death). Facing this approach, disorder has insidiously settled in his house otherwise so warm and welcoming; we eat at a table on which all the little tools of daily life can be found: matches, unemptied ashtrays, cases for glasses, envelopes, pencils, bills, books, corkscrews; greasy dust sticks to the tablecloth. It's difficult to find again the laughter from the past. The conversation is at once more superficial and sporadic. Facing these thickening shadows, we find ourselves destitute; also somewhat like assailed people who must economize their reserves.

(6 May)

Visit to Truinas. Comps as if lit up by the sunset. Herds of cows, some black and white, others copper-coloured.

The quince tree is growing onto the roof, the house will soon be devoured by the vegetation which creates, at this hour, an almost cold shadow. André has lost weight, he has a pale complexion and a seemingly thin mouth. Anne, who is as warm as ever, seems to have hardened features, straighter hair. He immediately wants to make a fire in the fireplace and brings long thin branches that he places very high over a bit of newspaper, so that the fire takes a long time to flare up.

During the conversation, following up on one of Anne's remarks about their visit to Prague, he comes out with a statement that is surprisingly harsh for him: that this remark reminds him of another one, which one Madame C. let slip in a salon, the stupidest remark he has ever overhead, he says: that is, that this woman, while others were speaking of death, apparently cried out: 'I love death', in the same tone that she might have used to say: 'I love port!' Sometimes, he visibly feels a sharp pain and makes a face to push it away. Then, three times, he will become slightly dizzy—as if, he explains, an intense hot flush were rising to his head—which leaves him speechless, with the extremely moving expression of a child surprised to discover pain or a truly sombre mystery. Just as soon afterwards, he insists on getting up, on serving himself some herb tea; after much effort. His health, based on what he has told us, is alarming.

(31 August)

On television, Julien Green at home, shrouded in the redness of his flat; if the show is recent, his presence of mind is exceptional, since he is ninety-seven years old. A character from another age: vest, tie, refined language, humour and extreme courtesy. He commands sympathy as much as he does admiration. Images from the First World War are shown, when he was a very young ambulance driver; the troops leave for the front with enthusiasm whereupon trenches, stretchers, shell holes, trees reduced to skeletons. Nausea when facing these absurdities that have incessantly begun again here and here ever since. Green, when he speaks about this, never abandons his level-headedness, never raises his voice, and simply says: 'Ever since then, I have known that I would always loathe war.' He says that when facing the fine, beautiful hands of a dead young soldier that are visible beyond the hood that has been drawn over the face.

The sentiment that all of this is definitely too onerous; lassitude; and the conviction that everything that I have been able to write is definitely so little, so frail; that I am not up to anything. But it is difficult to efface oneself completely. Anne de Staël's letter about André's health: 'a poet's true body is the body of words'—I have never believed that, and that is probably my weakness, my fault.

(16 October)

Turkey, *Istanbul*. For the Book Fair. Impressions as chaotic as the city itself, from which, to be truthful, I have retained little.

First of all, once again, I am tense, full of apprehension, with the nearly constant feeling that I will not show myself to be 'up to the occasion', which reduces my receptiveness: I will almost sense *at a distance* the things that we will see, some of them obviously admirable, and the people whom we will meet, one or two of whom are of especially high quality. This *distance*, as opposed to so many other trips in the past where some emotions were so deep.

A striking and probably (for me) distressing example: Hagia Sophia, which did not give me the expected and, apparently, habitual shock. This might have been caused by my mood; but by other reasons as well: the presence, beneath the dome, of the enormous scaffolding to help restore the dome and that spoils the inner volume of space; the restorations already finished, too neat and trivializing; the excessive grandeur, perhaps (as I experienced in Karnak), as opposed to what I recalled of the so-much-more-mysterious intimacy of Saint Mark's, in Venice; perhaps even the excessiveness of a luminosity which, conversely, has been much vaunted, notably by Duthuit? To the extent that I have especially kept the memories of the Deesis of the gallery, of such-and-such a square door with its simple marble cornices, and of the extraordinary colours of some big panels also made of marble.

Of the mosques, I will especially remember the great exterior beauty, notably of those resulting from the art of Sinan the architect: grey hills rising gently towards the sky. And those calm courtyards where the faithful carry out ritual ablutions. But the interiors often surprise, and disappoint, since they create so little sacred sentiment. Too many ornaments, too much light filtered through too-bright windowpanes, too much architectural foliage . . . and such little difference with the interiors of palaces, the ceremonial rooms of a harem. All of this flits about, like a bazar. They are prayer parlours, whatever might be the beauty of the details and, of course, of the earthenware. The only thing really able to move me is the severe, inventive and powerful beauty of some big ancient calligraphies.

(24 November)

1998

Eclecticism. I surprise myself by noting that, for several months now, I have had in front of me, leaning like playing cards—for a more gratuitous and serious game—against the little green volumes of Goethe's *Collected Works*: Poussin's *Blind Orion*, *The Pilgrims of Emmaus* of the Jacquemart-André Museum, the head of a Bodhisattva from the sixth or seventh century coming from Tumxuk and housed in the Guimet Museum, a Rothko—*Green and Maroon* on a blue background—from Washington; then *Room*, of a haiku poet, Kafū Nagai (?), showing a musical instrument, a flower, a written page, a panel decorated with a poem; and finally *Nachi Waterfall*, a work from the Kamakura period: so many proofs of beauty that are surprisingly varied, a true cupboard of a 'museum of the imagination'—and I don't deny it, since each of these works, in its own way, speaks to me, as if each had reached along its own path a peak where one breathes air so pure that it heals you of the words disillusionment.

I would therefore have wished to question them all; but I have nothing to say about some of them. From the pages written back then, I will thus retain only a few lines.

Poussin paints something like the music of the earth, the mute, deep music of foliage, clouds and mountains; blind Orion walks there like another mountain; the sky is the purest blue. The calmness of the landscape makes me think of Hölderlin's great poem, which begins: 'As when on his day of rest a farmer goes out . . .' (to inspect his fields after a storm). But it is also because of Greece: nothing is closer to the prose of *Hyperion* than these great, powerful and calm landscapes where demigods and nymphs are still in their right place; the unity of the world is still perceptible there as a respiration, for the last time perhaps in our Western world. (I also liked this painting because it reminded me of André du Bouchet, who spoke so well of it.)

Nachi Waterfall: it is difficult to speak of this hanging scroll painting, after Malraux. As he pointed out, it is not a waterfall; he compares it to a two-edged sword; in any case, it is no longer water. As for myself, especially sensitive to real waterfalls, I shouldn't even like this one which freezes them: actually, more than a two-edged sword, doesn't this painting evoke a part of a belt that had fallen straight down along a stone vestment? The comparison is not absolutely devoid of meaning, for in this art there is some of the hieratic elegance of traditional costumes, even something 'decorative'. An admirable work of art all the same, with, barely visible at the top, a star hardly less dark than the sky and the cliff boulders, and those few trees that are light green as if embroidered on the steep slopes. Seized by veneration in this place that was already sacred at the time, did the artist want to say: this waterfall that I see and that could splatter me if I got too near to it, that could also refresh me and quench my thirst, is a thing too beautiful to be imitated or even suggested in its veracity; to show its meaning, I must transmute it into a sign as if ice had frozen it: a white line crossing the dark page, as if someone had half-opened a curtain concealing a divinity? (As much as I admire this, I realize, merely by seeking out the words to express it, that all this remains a little strange to me, like that meticulous ceremonial of tea or those ritual flower arrangements that call for an almost military discipline, enough to make you flee to the other end of the earth or, more simply, into the first meadow you come across . . .)

(About Rembrandt's painting, nothing to say which would not risk repeating what I wrote in the past after a visit to the museum in Cologne.)

As to the head of Bodhisattva, if I have chosen it among so many others, I think that two reasons explain this and join in moving even the ignoramus that I am in this field: first, its material, 'dried earth, partly heated', a modest material that is rougher, more fragile than stone, marble or bronze, and is exposed to the wearing down of time and bad weather; so that the face, which is probably feminine, in any case juvenile, and lit up by a shy, very internalized smile, does not seem taken away from our world to revolve among the stars. The modesty of this material, therefore; and, second, the surprising ornamental richness of the kind of crown that surmounts the infinitely gentle face, framed by the marine-like undulations of the hair. And that kind of crown, or tiara, which is complicated, made of knots, rings, braids and big flowers, given that it has been sculpted in the same material—that comes down to us shaded with wear—as the head, far from overwhelming it, like those 'vain ornaments' of which Phèdre complains, seems, on the contrary, to be the final outcome, one whose pensive grace still deserves today to be paid tribute.

Rothko, *Green and Maroon* (1953): could it be that the bodhisattva, beneath his lowered eyes, contemplated something like this painting, which would convey to him his solemn calmness? Among so many so-called abstract paintings painted in this century, and especially after the war, and which are often so empty, mechanical, or outrageously aggressive, how did Rothko manage to communicate such a feeling of plenitude, more or less happy or dark depending on the periods, with this appearance of 'almost nothing'?

Kafū Nagai's *Room*: the haiku that appears there in its blue frame has been translated for me like this:

> 'The blue bamboo
> awaits him, bends, straightens up.
> Spring snow.'

All this would be vapid, too exquisite, were it not for his free, quick pen strokes that give the impression of coming across—in passing and without attaching too much importance to it—the condiments of a dish of which a mere trifle would make us taste the deep savour. One could also detect allusions to a secret life spotted through a window and that would suffice to measure the price of it. (For example, to glimpse a tortoiseshell comb and a mirror would be more moving than even the presence of the woman who has just used them, or will soon use them.)

There will have been a few moments in my life when I will have felt myself closer to that art than to any other, because it then seemed to me, in its very fragility, to be the least perishable.

*

[To my notes about Jacques Borel's *L'Effacement* (The Effacement), reproduced in *Carnets* (Notebooks), pp. 120–3, I could add these lines, deleted back then:]

Since Borel has remained a poet, whatever the appearances: 'What flowers to carry to this grave—or what ball, what lost hoop, what tin soldier lying in the grass back then?' (The grave of his too-beloved mother?) It is admirable, even if Rilke's poems 'written at the Ragaz cemetery' could have remotely inspired him. This presence of children—once again, as an echo of the 'green paradise of childhood loves' that is unforgotten, unforgettable—as, later on, of William Blake. Why thus wish, to this extent, to 'die lost', why feel 'degraded' by the thought of salvation?

In the chapter 'I did not know', echoing Perec's 'I remember' series, when he thinks back on that toy that he did not know, the 'teetotum', and, at the same time, on the marvellous Chardin of *Child with a Teetotum*, the thought of Mozart, suddenly, occurs to him: how right this comparison seems to me!

In 'The Rustling of the Dead', this simple sentence: 'What old living woman, when brushing up against this dress, or merely this imperceptible breath, have you once again brushed up against?' With these words, how close we are to Rilke, notably to his admirable 'Requiem for a Friend'!

And also this poignant question: 'A ghost, this rose in the air that you have, however, not stopped seeing blossoming?'

(If I recall correctly, we are almost twins; which is enough to take astrology seriously, at least for a moment...)

(16 January)

About embankment flowers: at the end of the walk— or at the stopping place, or whatever—those that move me the most are the most humble ones, growing along the ground—the well-known pink bindweed. It is a rather beautiful thing in that it grows just like that. But will I ever understand something about it one day or later? Before closing the book that one never reads well enough.

(14 September)

Invited by Switzerland to the Frankfurt Book Fair. What a traveller becomes today: an object more and more scheduled and canalized, circulating like a particle in the CERN linear-accelerator ring—the comparison is, indeed, more than approximate, though it has come to mind!—slipping cards into machines, going forward on conveyor belts, just like his baggage, checked in, taken over, 'dispatched' and so on. Before leaving, my knees ached in the stairways of our home in Grignan; there, I noticed that I had not found a stairway to climb until two days had gone by, at the Städel Museum.

In the four-star hotel, no one but impeccable gentlemen wearing ties, no one greeting anyone in the lift or elsewhere. No more need for an identity card: the credit card is the only worthwhile passport. A city of skyscrapers shiny like quartz, raising the money-king banner very high.

The sentiment that poetry is a thousand miles from all this, including the Fair with its literary-salon vanities.

But who knows if I am not still farther from some contemporary novelists than the CEOs with Vuitton or Hermès suitcases? Because those CEOs are who they are, men of money and power, and some writers would also like to be like that, with fame in addition— whereas literature should save what is essential but without thinking about it and, especially, without priding itself on it. (An incredible dialogue between Sollers and Houellebecq in *Le Nouvel Observateur*.)

Actually, the most truthful thing that I saw in Frankfurt was the 'Interiors' exposition at the Städel Museum, where the most simple, familiar reality had been explored and worked over by art to help it blossom and bear fruit: how a bedroom can be permeable outside, how a frame is not necessarily a prison; how the bedroom remains for us a central, sometimes radiant place. Even that battered wardrobe where Kabakov tells of having taken shelter when a child.

(17 October)

The doctor has given André du Bouchet three years to live. Should such a verdict be pronounced, or not?

On the telephone, with a weak voice, he confesses that he is completely worn out. This moves me all the more in that this kind of avowal is not characteristic of him.

(3 November)

Péguy, in his book *Le Porche du mystère de la deuxième vertu* (The Entrance to the Mystery of the Second Virtue), which will soon be one hundred years old:

'Thus the soul, that beast of ploughing, and of
    earthly ploughing,
Of a carnal ploughing . . .'

He also ploughs the page, slowly, incessantly, digging out furrows of verse poetry and Bible-like verse. Nothing can keep me from remaining sensitive to his voice.

Sometimes, when he resorts to great similes, we are reminded of the use Homer made of them, at the very beginning of 'our' poetry:

> 'Like the last of the peasant women, if the queen in her palace cannot feed the heir apparent,
> Because her milk has run dry,
> Then the last peasant woman of the last parish can be called to the palace . . .'

Later, when he gives voice to Hope:

> 'If it were with a pure soul that she made a pure soul,
> Of course, that wouldn't be clever. Anyone could do the same. And there would be no secret.
> But it's with dirty water, old water, tasteless water.
> But it's with an impure soul that she makes a pure soul and it's the most beautiful secret that exists in the garden of the world.'

Thereafter follows the very beautiful sequence of the Corpus Christi procession, with Hope like a tireless, impatient child:

> 'Twenty times she runs ahead, like a little dog, coming back, heading out again, twenty times covering the same path.
> [. . .]

> She never listens. She can't stand still at the
> altars of repose.'

Upon which the book concludes with a long 'Hymn to the Night' impregnated with confidence and pity.

(5 November)

Hopkins, 'To What Serves Mortal Beauty?':

> 'What do then? how meet beauty? Merely meet
> it, own,
> Home at heart, heaven's sweet gift; then leave,
> let that alone.
> Yea, wish that though, wish all, God's better
> beauty, grace.'

(24 November)

Péguy, in the last poem of *La Tapisserie de Notre-Dame* (The Tapestry of Notre-Dame), which an uncle gave to me as a gift in 1942, the 'Prière de report' (Prayer of Deferment):

> 'We no longer know anything of what was read
> to us,
> We no longer know anything of what was said
> to us,
> We know nothing but an eternal edict,
> We no longer know anything but your absolute
> order.'

Wouldn't someone in me wish to be able to repeat that, provided that the order really came from what is highest?

(25 November)

1999

First dream of the year.

As I watch our car heading up a steep slope, going near the edge of a cliff, I shout to my wife who, as usual, is driving, to be careful since the shoulder appears very soft; indeed, just afterwards, I see the soil crumbling away under the right-hand tyres and the ground giving way; at this point, I don't remember seeing the car toppling down but, following the accident, it is not Anne-Marie but my mother who has fallen to the foot of what looks like a groove vertically hollowed out in land by a waterfall; that is, all the way to the bottom of a sort of ravine from which it is urgent to recover her. My daughter is the first one to climb down this cliff; however, not heeding my advice to descend cautiously, she slips in turn, fortunately without hurting herself; while I, more prudent because I am more thoughtful, arrive without mishap near the hole where my mother has fallen and from which—it seems—we have managed to bring her out in time by lifting big cardboard-like slabs that had kept her partly concealed; even as machines, in a town devastated by an earthquake, can be seen lifting enormous concrete slabs beneath which survivors will hopefully be found.

It was not a very merry dream for the beginning of a year. It reminded me of the supplies of anxiety which we store inside ourselves and on which our nights draw chronically; all-too-justifiable anxieties that are sources for nightmares that do not always end so well.

That afternoon, I had gone to walk on the path that joins the stream called the Lez at the point where, a few years previously, had been established a rather modest sort of ranch that now needs to be crossed if one wants to continue walking. As always in wet weather, there was a lot of mud there, which did not make the walking very pleasant; in addition, still far from the entrance, I had been welcomed by barking dogs, two of which had not hesitated to race towards me, the first one big with dark fur and of an undetermined race, the other one very small, like a griffon, and I wondered if it might belong to some friends of ours who had gone there to have a horse ride—I didn't see exactly who they could be, however, but the thought reassured me a little; after which, as I was walking past the stables and a young man wearing boots emerged from the refreshment stand, without making the slightest sign towards me, another dog, a wolf-hound this time, the colour of dirty snow and also barking, but unaggressively, came over to sniff me; it was a sort of ghost dog. And since I had left home without my glasses, which is a very rare act of negligence on my part, I could not see anything as clearly as usual; the horses, especially, which had remained outside in their muddy enclosures beneath the dark trees, were not exactly as real as they should have been.

A little farther on, the path rises in such a way that the stream starts becoming visible from above. I noticed that it was flowing more or less normally, although there was not very much water, and that the grass and the low plants, which had recently grown, formed along the banks patches of an extremely dense and fresh green colour. There were no more walkers along this path than there had been people enjoying horse rides at the ranch.

Still farther on, the path, bordered by mossy ancient rock, keeps rising while distancing itself a little more from the stream; once again barking reached me, but from a farm this time; two dogs were running towards me while children were trying, in vain, to call them back. Beautiful sunlight was shining down on all this. At this point, since I was a little shaky on my feet from the previous day's festivities, I headed back down the path.

I thought of this very ordinary walk during the night, after my dream had ended; and I was surprised at how little it would have taken to make the narrative seem like another dream, with an admittedly less imposing yet palpable shade of anxiety, and with those passages over unsafe ground. Apart from the fact that the mud of the walk had left traces on my shoes, whereas I had no chance of finding any traces on me (if not 'in' me) of the accident in the dream.

At this moment in my life when all the things of this world were appearing more incomprehensible than ever before, this was not the first time I was dis-covering the rather blurred border between our dreams and real lives; nor I was surprised at the fair amount of unreality of the latter. Upon which the idea came to me—ever in the darkness of the night which, moreover, was nearly over yet in a confused, slower way because of the cloud cover—that I could just as well have invented a next episode in my walk; for example if, instead of heading home because we were expecting, at the end of the afternoon, friends with whom we were supposed to go and fete others, among the oldest and dearest whom we have here and who have unfortunately not been in very good health for some time now, I had continued to walk—instead of carrying out this amiable duty—, had passed by the farm from which the two hunting dogs had emerged, and, going down the path this time, had met up again with the stream in a wilder and more peaceful spot from which, downstream, the remains of a former railroad bridge can be made out. I would then have passed another person walking in the same direction and towards whom I would have turned without long glancing at him, just merely wishing him a Happy New Year; and this other person might have turned out to be a woman whom the walker, thereafter ceasing to be me, had known years beforehand and who would have invited him to have a drink at her house, not far from there, in that small village which overlooks the stream from its other bank and in which she had come to live. And perhaps then, forgetful of his duties ('I forgot all my human duties in order to follow him,' I then thought, recalling this declaration that Rimbaud lends to the 'foolish virgin' speaking of the 'infernal bridegroom' in *A Season in Hell*), the walker, now so far from everything, would have lost himself in the love of this woman whom he had run into once again. Or he would have noticed an old man like him seated on a stump and staring both attentively and vaguely at the water flowing by, and he would have spoken to him; this man (why not, now that I was inventing?) would have invited him to follow, to enter one of those caves, sometimes sheltering foxes or birds, that the water had hollowed out a very long time ago in cliffs which, in places, rise along the stream; and through this cave the walker, distancing himself little by little from the so-called real world, would have had access to vast luminous halls at the ends of which, as in one of Novalis' tales, he would have learnt secrets concerning the life and the death from which perhaps he, deep down inside himself, dreamt of escaping . . .

Then, still at the end of this night, I realized that this novel or this tale would constitute still another state of the 'world'; different from my real life and different from the dreams that come to you from that same life; more or less different, in fact, depending on whether I mixed a more or less large share of my memories, musings and desires into these fictive stories.

All the same, the walk had been real since it had left traces of real dirt on my shoes; the dream had taken place only 'in my head', even if this expression is not rigorous; in any case, it had occurred without my wishing it to take place and yet, after all, its dreamt mud might have left its invisible traces 'inside me'; moreover, it was an image of my real mother who had taken the place of my real wife at the moment of the accident. Whereas I would have deliberately invented the people encountered by the walker in any possible narrative, like the very story of which they would have been the protagonists; and I realized, quite obviously, that I could never *invent* any story, less by a lack of imagination than by a rejection of any kind of 'lying' . . .

To these three modes of experience—the real walk on which the weak sunlight that day was shining; the dream of the accident located in its own fashion inside me and surrounded by the darkness of the night and visible to no one else; and the fiction only sketched out, and also inside me, once I had awakened yet still in the night and no less invisible outside myself— would soon be added another: that of words traced on the page to translate all three modes, bring them together, reflect them, add them to so many others most of which have vanished like smoke and a few of which persist, in books, in our heads, and sometimes seem more to fortify the 'real' light than to uselessly distract our eyes.

(2 January)

A young Romanian woman student has taken the risk of drafting a master's thesis on 'Contemporary and Mystical Poetry' in which this poetry is restricted to two names, Celan and mine. One is never circumspect and rigorous enough when using the word 'mystical'. A genuine mystic burns with an ardour for God that can surely efface, when it reaches incandescence, the framework of dogma; he nonetheless knows for whom he burns and leads his life accordingly. It seems to me that such is an 'uprightness' straight like an arrow or a flame that goes far beyond even the purest élans of poets. I cannot speak of Celan, who is almost inaccessible in the great torment of his destiny; for me at least, I float outside of all religious frameworks in the greatest (the most pitiful?) uncertainty; and above all, I live like everyone else, an 'uomo qualunque' if there ever was one; simply, from time to time, nourished, comforted by intuitions that can vaguely resemble the spiritual ascensions of mystics—like the flickering flame of a candle in contrast to a lightning bolt or the splendour of the sun.

(15 January)

For a Yes or For a No by Nathalie Sarraute: an admirable performance of actors, indeed, but also of the writer stalking what lies beneath the surface of words and managing to make her stalking interesting, even sometimes moving. In her interview with Claude Régy, she herself appears a beautiful old lady infinitely worthy of respect; tranquil, without the slightest pose, warmly intelligent, to the extent of making me regret the severity of what I had written about her work long ago and making me wish to give the reading of her book a second try. Except that I already know what risks making me weary of those books: their abstraction (this is not the right word), the absence of the colours of this world and of human beings in their singularities. All that is, in contrast, in Chekhov, who was evoked in another radio show just afterwards, with more or less well-presented excerpts from his work, in which I found all that I have always liked for such a long time in his *oeuvre*: that 'reality' that leads you to laughter or the brink of tears, because we find ourselves in our own depths; whereas Sarraute, in her play, merely offered me a kind of analysis, indeed extremely subtle, deep and original, of a situation that nevertheless leaves the protagonists indifferent, they being neither Lopakhin, Ermolay nor Uncle Vanya, but H1 and H2.

This being said, how beautiful was that almost nonagenarian old lady, how moving and 'genuine'! I also liked the fact that she cited Baudelaire among her favourite authors. Why then must trees, the sky, hairstyles, the colours of eyes and so on, be excluded from such books? As if a too-sharp, too-suspicious mind, scalded by too many illusions, ceased to perceive them, or rejected them. (Except, as it seemed yesterday evening, moments of childhood?)

*

Petrarch, in a letter to Agapito Colonna, between 1338 and 1343: 'For life today has reached such a degree of crime and fury that one cannot take an extra footstep without causing general ruin.'

(20 January)

Leafing through a short essay collection by Alvaro Mutis, *Contextos para Maqroll* (Contexts for Maqroll), I am struck to read that he has never been able to read to the end of either of Miller's *Tropics*; and that to his eyes, the minute description of various sexual acts has nothing to do with genuine eroticism. To write this today must seem rather corny, but joins the sentiment that has long been mine in this respect. [Recently, in 2008, I discovered that Mutis was a very good, very sensual poet.]

(12 March)

How can a poet (Patrick Laupin, in the bulletin of the *Arald*) write like this today? 'This voracity of instinct, this principle of omnitude, which demands all rights for oneself and in which speaking words de-speaks, show that the primitive force of destruction can easily win over that of creating. If another place for writers is at stake, then it seems to me that this place dons the meaning to come of a stateless, navigating being who recreates the hesitating hieroglyph of his hearing and of his silence as well as by the deftness of this human way of speaking words that splits on the surface the usurious lucidity of symbols, perhaps thereby contributing to sign the especial insanity of identity logics.'

(9 June)

Borges.

Yesterday evening, I reread, aloud and with intense pleasure, the first three texts of *Fictions*, including the marvellous 'Pierre Ménard'. In this writer, through his extreme intellectual subtlety, I am moved by a kind of deep courtesy and cheerful melancholy, the soulful elegance of a grand gentleman lacking vanity—everything that comes to the surface more frankly in his poems.

(21 August)

Simone Weil's letter to Joë Bousquet: what density, what force, what intelligence! How can one dare to place the slightest thought alongside that letter which severely reminds you of your mediocrity of mind and soul.

But: how can one believe in the way she does? This is beyond me.

(13 September)

Jean-François Billeter, apropos of Chuang-Tzu (henceforth Zhuangzi): 'Philosophical reflection is more worthwhile, it seems to me, when it enables us to grasp, on the spot, our own ways of thinking and gives us, by this very means, the freedom of modifying them, if need be.'

In his analysis of the beginning of the collection *Tchouang-Tseu* (1994), he speaks of a necessary 'candour', of 'the total absence of intention' that alone allows the right vision and can be given to outcasts—which inevitably reminds me of Dhôtel's characters.

On the language and the world, on the 'unchanging reality' such as Giacometti sensed on the Atlantic Ocean—and which recalls my own impressions of crossing the ocean—Billeter quotes the sculptor: 'And then what can I say in the middle of this endless, nameless ocean, in the middle of this black water into which I could sink, in which I could be eaten, devoured, by blind, nameless fish . . .'

The conclusion of the study, on the sage's attitude toward language, makes me think that mine, with regards to poetic labours, is not all that far removed. (Or would I be, in this respect, too pretentious?)

(24 September)

In regard to my text on the colours of evening 'when coming back from the Val des Nymphes'—something I have never seen elsewhere—it occurs to me that the incapacity to express colours is more obvious than any other analogous case. The progression remains (dangerously, unfortunately?) the same: observations as precise as possible (à la Francis Ponge, but without the humour), as complete in certain respects for some of them, and accurate; then, when one has realized that thereby, *nothing has been said*, the stepping back, the unbridling of the imagination, of reverie; finally ('finally' is not the word), a more or less bold intuition that forgets the specific accumulated notes, more or less taken back up and revised, and seems to open up a path which, in the final reckoning, is 'truer'; but sometimes too general, so that the path could be understood as an evasion or, worse, as a sleight of hand.

And if I endeavoured to 'think' a little? . . . First, such encounters are relatively rare, and linked to precise circumstances involving the place, the season, even sometimes the hour. For example, I only saw there (twice, unless I am mistaken, at the beginning and the end of winter), nowhere else, the colours of which I tried to define the effect and to understand the sense. Second, such encounters do not seem linked to a particular mood that might have been mine at the time—except for a general state of vague availability. *Yet they are always surprises*, thus unexpected, undeserved if you will, and kinds of gifts, or better: grace given by the world. Denied, therefore, more or less, to the observer of nature, to one who is on the lookout; 'oblique', as it were, reaching you from the side instead of head-on—while you were thinking of something completely different, or of nothing. The encounters are not given by slowness, meditation or asceticism, nor do they presuppose any 'technique' (of breathing, concentration, forgetting what is contingent, etc.); they would hardly even demand having the mind free. Gifts all the more welcome, all the better received in that they come without conditions, or almost. To be the beneficiary, one will have had no need to pray, to have given first, even less so to have paid something (one might as well say that it is almost 'too beautiful').

(Ideally, in fact, one would not speak about them, comment on them, nor revolve around them: merely make them sparkle quickly.)

Having reached this point, I must constrain myself to 'thinking' a little more, even without great hopes of being successful.

In this particular case, what has surprised the eyes? The rareness, the strangeness of what has been perceived in passing: that is, colours *other* than they usually are, elsewhere; and because of them, a brief metamorphosis from a completely common piece of landscape whose elements change—for the eyes, by no means inside the elements themselves—in their nature, no longer appearing completely themselves, or 'only' themselves; perhaps it should be said: a little less 'real', or a little less univocal, delimited, closed in. But why is this impression, which is hardly conscious at the moment, of seeing the elements changed, so surprising and, moreover, heartening? For they could have undergone a transformation—apparent, once again—that would be worrisome, even frightening, as when clouds start looking like monsters, or when—this time in reality—something spoils, deteriorates, decomposes. However, it is the opposite that has happened. The elements have not become 'more beautiful': they seem to *speak another language* than everyday language . . .

When this rather accurate impression, which I have noted, of 'shifting from one space to another', yet in a rarer and thus more surprising way, than by effects of fog or rain. (The difficulty to define this experience is definitely very great, especially if I wish to be wary of ingeniousness.)

What a strange idea, if one thinks about it, to rejoice in this; in such trifles, and in what is obviously a pure illusion! Yet which, all the same, has happened: a mirage is something as a mirage; an illusion is real in its own way, as an illusion. To keep working time and time again on this issue, whereas elsewhere so many human beings cannot do so yet are numbed by their misfortune, whatever it is—yet which, alas, has nothing of an illusion to it! An old song, like my attempt at a response: not all the attention must be given to misfortune. Otherwise, one might just as well head for the beyond.

In the order of nature, it is obviously a matter of light. Well, this should also be so in the order of the mind. A sort of enchantment aroused by the means of matter, purely by chance, without any consequences for the natural order—even as the night changes nothing, or almost, to those meadows, those trees, or those hedges that can be found as such, the next morning.

Light, in this brief moment at the end of day— and at the end of winter—has shown imagination, has created an image, as poets sometimes manage to do. But, between many invented and proposed images, some affect us more than others, and others not at all. When they affect us in this way, it is because they have thus done your work, as it were, invented, instead of you or before you, an image, perhaps a scene, of which you hadn't even had an idea, whereas it was waiting deep inside you, somehow, to be brought to light. Indeed, it seems the world has gone to seek inside you a vague but deep reverie and give it a form for an instant, without shouting 'look out'.

There would thus be there an analogy with the images of our dreams, which are also, but in a different way, of the order of the unreal, which does not prevent them from existing, nor from having meaning and worth.

Henceforth, I could understand why a too-minute analysis of their components could risk destroying them and, at best, betraying them; whereas more freely evoking the effect gives the impression that one is closer to the 'truth' which, above all, it matters to you to near.

(Thus, when I evoked in my text 'a servant woman who invites you to come in', to enter another space—the means used by the supposed magician to produce this effect perhaps having—but is this entirely certain?—little importance.)

It was also, and I must not forget this, that very mysterious moment between day and night, between winter and spring . . . and suddenly, I remember *La Cantate à trois voix* (The Cantata in Three Voices), 'that hour between spring and summer', and already in that great poem, that hour had given rise to the presence of women, no less than three of whom were needed to express the moment; and if I liked that book so much, it could not have been by pure chance.

(Noon and midnight have something fixed, absolute, about them: the peak of the day and the peak of the night. 'Noon the righteous weaves the sea of fires / The sea, the sea ever beginning again . . .' This shows that a few lines of verse, even Valéry's, are engraved in my memory.)

(18–19 November)

On 19 March 1827, Goethe writes to Zelter: 'The circle of my intimate friends appears to me as a bundle of Sibylline pages which, one after another, consumed by the flames of life, are scattered into the air, thus lending to the survivors a value that increases from moment to moment . . .' After which he adds: 'Let's keep active until that moment when, called back by the Spirit of the world, some earlier, some later, we will return to Ether!'

(The metaphor of the 'Sibylline pages' alludes to the story of Lucius Tarquinius Superbus and the Cumaean Sibyl. The latter wanted to sell the nine volumes of the 'Sibylline Books'—a collection of Greek oracles—to the king, who found the price too high; the Sibyl then burned, in front of him, the six first volumes, until the king accepted to pay for the last three, at the price for all nine. Goethe found in this story a metaphor of the value of life. As to myself, when I heard these words, 'Sibylline pages', I imagined only that the Sibyl scattered the oracles in the wind like pieces of paper. I must verify this.)

Virgil, in the sixth book of *The Aeneid*, has Aeneas say this to the Sibyl, to whom he has come to consult: 'Simply, don't confide your prophetic verses to pieces of paper that could be blown upwards in disorder, playthings of gusts of wind (*rapidis ludibria ventis*)'. A tradition behind this topic thus existed.

*

Mendelssohn, to whose piano playing Goethe much liked to listen to, writes to his parents on 25 May 1830: 'Every morning, I need to play the piano for an hour for him, running by all the great composers in alphabetical order, and explaining how each developed his style; he sits in a dark corner, like a *Jupiter tonans*, his old eyes shooting out lightning bolts [Goethe was eighty-one years old at the time]. He absolutely refused to get into the Beethoven. I told him that I couldn't help him out in that case, and played for him the first movement of the Fifth Symphony. He was strangely affected. First, he said: "This doesn't move whatsoever, it only surprises; it's grandiose." After which he mumbled something and started speaking again: "It's very great, completely insane, you could almost fear that the house would come crashing down. And when it's played by an entire orchestra! . . ."'

(20 November)

The evening light, like a hand passing over things to reassure them, to rescue them; so different from morning light.

(30 November)

The 'great music', the 'great organs' of Milosz have put into form a sort of emotion that is latent in us even if we have never experienced the circumstances: the return, at the end of life, to the childhood home, the painful measuring of the time gone by, the melancholy of autumn lingering like mist across a vast landscape— and this without his swelling his voice, rather as if he kept turning over, for himself, a complaint without feebleness.

(3 December)

While rereading the French poets of the twentieth century, many of whom no longer interest me, suddenly, leafing through the Pléiade edition of Supervielle: as, right away, he moves me, seemingly still alive, just as I had the chance to see him one single time, at his place, in front of Rogi André's lens, reciting one or two of his poems to make time go by! The text that stopped me short was 'À une enfant' (To a Young Girl), in which he speaks so tenderly to his daughter; and in which I immediately recognized one who speaks genuinely, without playing with words, without raising his voice more than is needed.

Hardly farther, it's in *Gravitations*, the last line of 'Grenade' (Pomegranate):

'[Nothing the fountains can do helps,]
The water that flows to console'

It's a fine example of his art: draw magic out of the most ordinary words.

(8–10 December)

2000

During Alain Finkielkraut's radio show *Répliques*, in which two historians of contemporary art were participating, one of them exclaimed: 'Well, we are indeed not going to speak about beauty, about the sublime', to which Finkielkraut responded, though almost in an aside: 'Why shouldn't we?'

Indeed, it's a surprising fact that the word 'beautiful' thus seems to be generally prohibited, and specifically when one is speaking about art. However, this word comes from further back than any theory; it rises to our lips spontaneously, in front of a landscape for example, without our even being able to imagine calling it into doubt, without our having to wonder what it means.

Even more so at a concert, at a museum, or in our reading. We have not yet started seeking out, in cities, the ugliest monuments or quarters, nor wishing to hear at a concert what we would like the least. Even if the notion of beauty has changed and will continue to change. I have myself happened upon the 'sublime' and not been able to find a better word to try to qualify what I had thereby encountered, and I stand by this experience.

What would one say of a race of 'new gourmets' who were seeking the worst possible cuisine and were rejecting the use of the word 'good'?

(8 January)

For my anthology project, and just to be sure, I reread Michel Leiris's *Haut Mal*, without much pleasure. I met him only once, rather bizarrely in fact, at the burial of one of my aunts, the mother of Annette Giacometti; she was also a widow and ill, he had very kindly taken her on a holiday on the shore of Lake Lucerne; a holiday interrupted precisely because of that ceremony, at the conclusion of which I found myself sitting next to him at a table in a sort of tearoom in Geneva. He then reminded me that I had been very reserved when judging his poetry; moreover, without acrimony, but with some apparent sadness. (In any case, he had not forgotten the review, after all the years that had gone by. At least I was able to tell him again how much I admired *The Rules of the Game*— but would I reread it, today?)

(25 February)

Funeral of our old friend Wayland Dobson in Réauville. The sunlight on the harpsichord keyboard, the lighted candles, the flowers, a homely full of warmth and simplicity pronounced by a priest who didn't know him, and especially, a 'ground' by Purcell that sounded admirably well when played by Patrick Ayrton. We were all very moved when we listened to it.

(9 March)

Frénaud: a poet whom I have perhaps not read well enough. But I had much liked, during the war, his *Rois mages* (The Magi); and today, I am pleased to quote the end of the 'Étape dans la clairière' (A Halt in the Clearing), from 1964:

> 'A party of daisies in the clearing.
> A frail paradise amid the shelter of willows.
> Water gently would cover us over, tiny seeds.
> Here is where I would like to vanish
> at this moment when the world is good.'

(10 March)

Rereading Robert Marteau's *Liturgie* (Liturgy) which, if he were not alive—but he is, fortunately— would find its place in my selection, for he is unjustly neglected; I would have no trouble choosing some of his very beautiful poems, when the description is not too 'visible'. Such as the one beginning with these lines:

'Who would know how to say it's beautiful like
    the berry
of the wild rose . . .'

Or this one:

'The holy ghost is everywhere: it can be
    heard in the oaks . . .'

(2 June)

In the *Anthologie de la poésie allemande* (Pléiade edition), I need to retain the adaptation, by Quirinus Kuhlmann (1651–89) whose *Kühlpsalter* Celan gave me as a gift, of Saint John of the Cross' poem 'En una noche oscura' (One Dark Night), especially the end, that last strophe with the enigmatic mentioning of Aminadab that had fascinated me:

'Zu Felses Höhlen Höhen
Eiln wir zugleich still zum Granatmoosstein.
Des Feindes sein Vergehen
Entlägert uns. Das Feld ist rein.
Der Wasser Schall macht Alles dein und mein.'

[To the boulders, the caves, the heights,
Let's run peacefully to drink pomegranate
    must.
With the enemy gone,
the siege is lifted. The field is pure.

The noise of the water makes the All yours and
    mine.]
(18 August)

Soon the hunting season will open: we come across
partridges on the path to the hill, and Orion already
appears at the end of the night.

A dream: a bird has alighted on a sort of stand in
a shed adjoining 'our' house—which has nothing to
do with the real house; a grey-feathered bird, rather
big, with a wing on only one side of its body (later, I
would realize that it looked more like a feathered
fish, rather ugly in fact, almost frightening); I had
just identified it as a nightjar when, strangely, it began
to speak to me, apparently to complain—perhaps
because of the hunters? I mention my stupor to those
close to me—seemingly, my son and wife—and I am
exasperated that they do not share it.

Another night, after a dinner washed down with
too much wine: I hesitate to note down a frightening
nightmare in which my father kept vomiting; and, at
a given moment, I noticed a doorway or at a tramway
door, two or three women coming out, in pink satin
dresses and looking genuinely like whores.

At the end of the dream, seeing a whole row of
rather poor people bent over to vomit as well, I told
myself that I was in Russia, in a place as wretched as

they were, the ground being very white, probably with snow.

(23 August)

The discovery, in a series published by Fayard, of the beautiful poems of Adam Zagajewski, confirms my idea that only poets from Eastern Europe, or almost, know how to speak of pain in a true and genuine tone, without rhetoric, without pathos, but without vain brutality as well. Like Holan, like Zbigniew Herbert, not to mention the great Russians.

'Tart Cherries, Sweet Cherries'

(In accounts of Franz Kafka's and Witold Gombrowicz's last days, one detail is repeated: the fruit they asked for)

Sweet cherries don't know who sends them.
Dark, tart cherries, soft, conceal their pits
inside, reminding us that the boundaries of things
sometimes dwell deep within them.
They comfort dying poets.
The gods of death recognize pity,
although they can't pronounce the word too soon.
They just send round, purple fruits
like leaves, furled and full of juice,
instead of letters.

(23 October)

Yesterday, a visit to André du Bouchet, surprisingly valiant, and as warm as ever, as sharp in his judgements.

'The voice
must not wallow'

he writes in *Annotations sur l'espace* (Carnet 3) (Annotations on Space [Notebook 3]).

(2 November)

2001

The Andante of Mozart's *Concerto Jeunhomme* as played by Clara Haskil (with Jochum as the orchestra conductor): As if a waterfall were reverberating, incorporating into its light the dark earth into which it sinks? As if its luminosity were full of low shadows, of complaints that it would make, through its plummeting downward, rise, and that it would transfigure? Waterfall, Jacob's ladder.

(23 February)

The afternoon of 29 March, Palézieux tells me on the telephone that Michel Rossier has died.

On 19 April, Anne telephones me to say that André died that morning at nine o'clock.

*

Senancour. Already a long time ago, in *Landscapes with Absent Figures*, I placed an entire chapter, essential to my mind, under his fraternal patronage. I came back to him in *Truinas, 21 April 2001* and, even more recently, at the end of *These Slight Noises*, to compare him to Leopardi. But of his *Rêveries* (Reveries) from 1803, which are thus anterior to *Oberman* and which I discovered only in the 2001 edition—to which I did not see without pleasure associated the name of Marie du Bouchet—I must absolutely retain here a few passages, among so many others that have deeply moved me through—for once, I will not refrain from using a word that has become trite today—a sort of musical magic.

Violets: 'an effortless emanation that would be disturbed by the slightest stirring of the air; a good that offers itself and escapes without moving off; the idea of a young girl who is your friend and still uncertain, yet pensive and naturally generous. [. . .] The violet belongs to contentment; it blossoms especially on slopes facing the south, not far from dabbling water.' These first notes (such is the right word), govern the movement titled 'Rest': 'Wandering water was flowing down into meadows already stripped of flowers.'

Wouldn't the most secret charm of a dream home be this one? 'A current of water was flowing through the house'—a marvel that I had actually seen in the Portuguese convent of Alcobaça.

This, too, more than a century before Proust: 'Some sadness is generally blended with the impression that can be made by voices placed at a great distance, and variable like moving air. This moving off into the distance recalls that of time, and it seems that these voices also leave us forever: as they fade away they renew the vague sentiment of our loses. If, on the contrary, during the ardour of the day, we happen to relax, at the end of a park in front of fields and meadows the few labours on which interrupt the silence, it is no longer things that move off: we ourselves abandon them. By gently forgetting them, we leave them behind for a more certain rest, and of this so-short minute will remain a memory which, now and then, will show up in all its power during the fruitful season. Sometimes, as we enter a deeper sleep, at the very instant that we are passing into it, there is for us a stroke of light, a trace of happiness, a glimpse whose fleeting quickness alone marks the boundary of the immensity. This seems foreign to everything that we know, foreign to everything that gives passion; this comes to us from absolute knowledge, from unlimited affection. Will our being detached from our present lives be like this at the ultimate moment of our tiredness on the earth?'

In the 'Infinite' chapter, these lines that Leopardi could have signed: 'Is there anyone who has not heard the threats of death? Death is present, it affects us. Our arts exist only through death, and our joys increase its attacks. We have an instant of life, to be the agents of death: our feet trample its victims, and our aspiration swallows them. When we celebrate our successes, we are clothed in debris, nourished by debris, sitting on debris. The hand, whose solemn gesture indicates sometimes incorruptible dwelling places, is also responsible for blessing those who are mustered by the banner of battle on the field of death. In the middle of our most pleasant countrysides, cleared by men who since then have died, rise our basilicas built by those same men, and capitals that they made lovely. They prepared our splendour; their sacrifices form our pride today, and often it is from our last day that we ourselves expect a kind of less fleeting existence.'

And farther on: 'A cloud of dust disturbs our gaze and conceals the infinite. [. . .] Long traces of destruction crisscross space. Near us, the water rising in invisible steam falls back down in heavy drops, and everywhere the movement of things, secretly reproduced, merely seems to be a perpetual collapse.'

(25 May)

Schlegel, quoted in Jean-Christophe Bailly's *La Légende dispersée* (The Scattered Legend), a very fine anthology of German Romantics: 'Blossoming is the joy of trees. How admirable Pliny's expression is! If a modern naturalist had coined it, we could congratulate him. It would be a sign that the sentiment of universal life in nature, of the soul of the world, had awakened in him.'

(7 June)

19 December: the death of Sebald, in a car accident, is announced. He was only fifty-seven years old.

One of the few 'new' writers who has totally won me over.

(19 December)

2002

I foresee, in a dream, the tribute to Bernard Simeone in which I will participate in a month in Lyon. I seem to have spoken with much warmth and that I will only have to repeat myself that day. Taking off from his pages about Pienza, where he meets up with Mario Luzi again, evoking the tension of his poetry, including heartrending passages; then, more extensively, about the fabric of *Cavatine* (Cavatina), like that of coat that would protect us as long as we are making it, but that would subsequently shrink to the extent that the author would even find himself naked at the end. All the same: the coat can later be worn by others, the readers. And this is not insignificant.

(9 January)

The beautiful anonymous text of the fifteenth or six-teenth century that Stravinsky used in his *Cantata* (1965); notably the text of the funeral vigil, from which these lines in Old English:

Strophe I
'This ae nighte, this ae nighte,
Every nighte and alle,

Fire and sleete and candlelight;
And Christe receive thye saule.

When thou from hence away are past,
Every nighte and alle,
To Whinnymuir thou com'st at last;
And Christe receive thye saule.'

And the Versus IV:

'If ever thou gav'st meat or drink,
Every nighte and alle,
The fire shall never make thee shrink;
And Christe receive thye saule.

If meat or drinke thou never gav'st nane,
Every nighte and alle,
The fire will burn thee to the bare bane;
And Christe receive thye saule.'

(The fire, the sleet, the snow—and the lit candle.)

(11 March)

Once again, unless I am mistaken, I am pleased to
quote these lines from Yeats' poem 'Vacillations', so
well translated by Bonnefoy:

'Un champ gonflé d'eau sous ses pas,
L'odeur du foin frais coupé
Dans son nez, le prince de Chou
S'écrira, désilluminant

La neige de la montagne:
"Que toutes choses s'éffacent!" '

[A rivery field spread out below,
An odour of the new-mown hay
In his nostrils, the great lord of Chou
Cried, casting off the mountain snow
'Let all things pass away']

(3 April)

Listened to Moulinié's *L'Humaine Comédie* (The Human Comedy) in a beautiful interpretation. 'Por la verde orilla del claro Tormes', 'va corriendo la niña' ('On the green shore of the clear Tormes, the girl is running'), a poem that one could daydream of rewriting in one's own manner, carried away by the spirit and the elation of the music. The tambourines. And all around, the tall oaks denser and denser with foliage.

*

Kafka. [Like Senancour, I give him his right place in *These Slight Noises*. But, among all that I have recopied, I still retain this:]

'Many are the shades of the dead who uniquely busy themselves with licking the waves of the river of death, because it comes from here and still has the salty taste of our oceans.'

(10 October 1917)

(I think of 'Regret de la terre', The Earth's Regret, Supervielle's poem of a completely different beauty.)

'The thorn-bush is the old obstacle on your path. If you want to go farther, it must catch fire.'

(18 November 1917)

In the second volume [of the Pléiade edition], which alludes to the story of the prodigal son: 'The longer one hesitates before the door, the more one becomes a foreigner.' Admirable prose, as is Gracchus the Hunter, in its extraordinary tranquillity of tone, wherein shines the memory of his stay in Riva, with these rare pleasant images:

> 'Have escaped them. By some kind of deft leap. At home, near the lamp, in my silent room. It's imprudent to say so. It calls them come out of the woods, as if the lamp had been lit to help them find the trail.' (5 February 1922)

(20 July)

Dream. I learn that Madame de R., the widow of a friendly philosopher with an orientalist bent, whom we would meet here once in a blue moon, is readying to leave on a trip. I decide to pay him a visit, at her place, before his departure; she lives in a big beautiful house in a nearby town. (This idea would never have occurred to me in reality, since our ties were not very close.) Once I have entered the house, I come across three women with veiled faces, wearing the long ecru-coloured garments of cloistered nuns; three tall creatures who remain absolutely speechless when I explain the reason for my coming. I am nearly certain, however, that one of the women is Madame de R.

After this, I go out and find myself in a kind of park that includes an esplanade, then some sloping ground, planted with trees among which must be pines or spruces: a rather austere place, as are, moreover, the actual house and garden of the couple. There are a lot of people who have apparently come to celebrate this departure, all of them silent as well, as least to me, to the extent that they could be suspected of belonging to some sect, but with nothing of the ridiculousness that can be associated with this image; instead, people exactly as our friends have been: serious, intelligent, music-loving, serene, distinguished. . .

Then, among these people scattered about the park, I notice a couple sitting at the edge of the slope, one of whom is wearing a mask; and when he takes it off, appears the face of man marked by poverty or alcohol.

This dream is not very significant, except for the image of those three tall entirely veiled women who had a statuesque beauty, in the bare room I had entered; or better, figures of a slow speechless choreography.

(25 November)

2005

Scève: I find him in the *Anthologie de la poésie française du XVIᵉ siècle* in the Poésie-Gallimard series.

Indeed, 'there is nothing new under [my] sun': I have barely left a Japanese poet from the twelfth century (*Ce peu de bruits*, pp. 108–12) and I find a sixteenth-century French poet from Lyon and, through him, that Góngora whose poetry had its hold on me almost as much as haiku, although one could think that the two genres are incompatible.

Scève, who is a genius of 'compactness', whereas the Japanese are geniuses of 'porousness', makes every dizain of his *Délie* a small edifice of solidly assembled words, cemented to the extent that one could fear having difficulty breathing in them, this being true from the end of the first poem that measures the blow received by the poet from his Lady's gaze:

'Great was the blow that, without cutting blade
The Body living still, kills the Spirit,
A pitiful victim in your admirable presence,
    Lady,
Fixed Idol of my life.'

The last line often being the crown of the pediment or, to venture another metaphor, the finely worked key to close a very precious jewel box; as is seen in dizain 148, the *n*th variation on the theme of seasons:

> 'Thus I in your ungracious frost am lean,
> My hopes are stripped of foliage in the cold;
> Then gentle spring returns with air less keen
> Superb in April my year begins to unfold.'

Something completely different thus commands admiration here; and it is not simple verbal virtuosity, no more than in the most beautiful passages of Góngora who can produce in us what must be called a kind of *joy*. It is, rather, a mastery such as it sounds as a high and proud defiance in regard to any form of disorder; one would think that such poets grasped tightly in their fist the weapon who shininess scares, and dispels the worst fears:

> 'White Dawn had barely finished crowning
> Her head with gleaming gold, & roses,
> When my Spirit, utterly foundering
> In the chaos of all it supposes,
> Now behind the Curtains which enclose it,
> Returned to render me less exposed to Death.
>
> But you, who (all alone) have the power
> To augur well for my fatality,

You will be the incorruptible Myrrh
Against the worms of my mortality.'

(25 February)

I am almost proud of having managed to read from
beginning to end Jean-Christophe Bailly's *Le Champ
mimétique* (The Mimetic Field), a very scholarly,
dense, rich but sensitive book on the Grecian world.
One of those books from which one would like to
retain a great many things. At heart, it is an essay on
the gradual distancing of the gods, the advance of
reason—but not any kind of reason—the movement
that leads from darkness to the clearness of daylight,
from savagery to appeasement, even as, in Aeschylus,
one moves from the Erinyes to the Eumenides.

It would be necessary to cite all the pages that
revolve around the 'Unswept House' mosaics made
by Sosus of Pergamon, the floor of a room covered
with the remains of a feast, the lowest among the 'low
subjects' about which speaks Pliny. Bailly writes:
'What moves us with these subjects [. . .] is existence:
neither as a proof nor as a trace, but as a deposit, or as
sleep. It is existence according to the truth that shines
forth in the absence of intention or of ostentation.'
And it is also that 'succo dei frutti caduti allora' of
which speaks Pavese in a poem from *Work's Tiring*:
'The juice from fruit that fell in those days' and, with

it, the bending beneath the air of time of what places itself, through the image, beyond time.'

Farther on, apropos of the 'famous enigmatic smiles of the korai', in opposition to Deonna who explains it as an inability of artists back then to create psychological nuances in living expressions, these admirable lines:

> 'There is no question of expressing anything whatsoever with these statues: they tell nothing, they figure in no narrative plot, they are the integral gestures, the prudent signs, that man, unbound from fright, addresses to the divinity. [. . .] The statue offered to the god smiles to the god; this smile is its prayer, its endeavour. In the space of the new religious relation that is formed, where the god is moving away, the statue, which stands before him and then takes a step towards him, retains him . . .'

(There are pages and pages that I would like to have shine forth here in their depth and measure, so worthy of their subject matter.)

And so many remarks, analyses whose subtlety astounded me, touched so closely some of my main, ever-too-vague intuitions! For example, when Bailly broaches on the creation of the city as an anti-labyrinth, and when, evoking the roles of columns, he quotes

Hegel: 'Columns support and delimit, but they do not form an enclosing wall', how could I not see again 'my' poplar groves in the Po Plain and so many of 'my' orchards, those permeable enclosures? Similarly, when he takes up the subject of the *interval* which creates order and is 'child of the unlimited', and which punctuates so well the sky that Plotinus can write: 'Stars are like letters forever being written in the sky, or like letters written once and for all and yet forever moving . . .'

And how could I not be happy that the book, tackling modern art in its last section, chooses Giacometti for its main figure?

> ' "God is dead" means nothing else than that: no longer the invisible, of any kind, holds the key that would rule distances in a visible considered, in any case, as a simulacrum. This also amounts to saying that there are no more simulacrums, nor, moreover, voices or oracles which would come to us from another, otherwise unattainable, side: everything has been attained, and it is because everything has been attained, is attainable, extinguishable, that everything, simultaneously, conceals itself.'

(2–13 September)

A book read 'by chance' that is timely: *Gestern unter-wegs* (Yesterday, Underway), Handke's notebook from the years 1987–1990. At his best, isn't Handke a remote descendent of Bashō, yet without any trace of imitation, of 'Japonism' or 'zenism'? Those tireless hikes almost with no other baggage then a good pair of shoes, a few books and the indispensable alliance of notebooks and a pencil, and this infinite capacity for astonishment and admiration, his unbelievably sharp eyes and also that 'heart', all the same, whereas one could be tempted, having seen him a few times, to judge him an egocentric.

*

Yesterday evening, while listening again to Bach's *English Suites* played by Leonhardt, I again find myself carried off by the élan of these pieces, which is not a 'dancing' élan despite their title and the origin of their forms; I think in turn of mobile houses, of mobile figures, of ornate time, whose structures would have become visible in the transparency of hearing; and also, because of the special sonority of the harpsi-chord, as I had already done so in my poems 'to Henry Purcell', of dialogues between icy peaks exchanging their scintillating reflections. At the same time, out-side, I see the recently denuded branches of the fig tree.

The prelude of the 'Third Suite': like so many waves, of sonorous troops climbing with enthusiasm and constancy to assail the most insurmountable, darkest rampart.

And, still immersed in the same listening experience, to complicate or, rather, enhance the synaesthesia— a phenomenon to which Handke often returns in his book, which will perhaps have opened up the access for me—I see the catalogue cover, from the last Poussin exhibition, with a detail from the marvellous *The Empire of Flora*, in Dresden, the gracefulness of the young goddess, the garlands behind her and the cluster of grapes in her hand. Garlands and clusters of grapes: they also pertain to this music which inebriates and delights the numbers, which runs without a spirit of conquest a race that has a meaning more than a goal— like that of streams which I will have so often liked to follow with my eyes.

Upon which I open the garden door to close the shutters and spot Venus, which has been particularly luminous these past few days, Mars like fire on the other side of the sky; I see Venus again as I have no longer had eyes for her for too long a time, shrill like a shrill note, like the song of a lark—or like in Mallarmé's poem:

'the bird that one never hears
another time in one's life'

And thinking back on all that, I meet up once again with Roud—as if I came across him miraculously in his 'lost countrysides': because of his sentences formerly known by heart from his *Essay for a Paradise*, which evokes his 'unheard-of' (I think it is indeed the word he uses) encounters, among which the 7th Fugue of the *Well-Tempered Harpsichord I* and, indeed, the Poussin who painted *The Funeral of Phocion* (which, moreover, inspired one of Bertolucci's most beautiful poems). With the musician as with the painter, what gratifies us is, apparently, an *order*, a supreme equilibrium that is neither imperious nor overwhelming (as I sometimes sensed, in situ, with ancient Egypt); an order, with Bach, willingly jubilant, more severe with Poussin (yet not in *The Empire of Flora*), with whom one sometimes walks like Orion in the mountains.

(21 September)

[And today, Friday, 13 March 2009, as I finish up, not without relief, the copy of this selection in a half-century of notebooks, I am pleased that it ends thus, with the dancing figure of Flora and so far from our debacles.]

Translator's Notes

Unless otherwise noted, all translations in this book are mine. In the case of French translations made or cited by Jaccottet, I have gone back, whenever possible, to the original sources and translated directly from them. For the following notes, I have used those included in the original French edition, *Taches de soleil, ou d'ombre* (Éditions Le Bruit du temps, 2013), sometimes providing additional information for the non-French reader. And I have added many other notes to elucidate references and allusions. I have also made use of the notes in the Gallimard-Pléiade edition of Jaccottet's *Oeuvres* (2014).

PAGE VII | The three *Seedtime* volumes: *La Semaison: Carnets 1954–1979* (Paris: Gallimard, 1984); *La Seconde Semaison: Carnets 1980–1994* (Paris: Gallimard, 1996); *Carnets 1995–1998* (*La Semaison, III*) (Paris: Gallimard, 2001). *Observations et autres notes anciennes* (*1947–1962*) (Gallimard, 1998). In English, the first two *Seedtime* volumes are available in Tess Lewis' translations at Seagull Books: *Seedtime* (2013), *The Second Seedtime* (2017).

PAGE 2 | Gustave Roud (1897–1976), Swiss poet and writer whose *oeuvre* was important for Jaccottet's literary coming of age. See *Philippe Jaccottet–Gustave Roud: Correspondance 1942–1976* (José-Flore Tappy ed., Paris: Gallimard, 2002) as well as Jaccottet's critical work, *Gustave Roud* (Fribourg: Éditions Universitaires de Fribourg, 1968, 2002). Roud lived in and wrote about the Jorat region of Switzerland. See his '*Air of Solitude*' *followed by* '*Requiem*' (Alexander Dickow and Sean T. Reynolds trans) published by Seagull Books in 2020.

PAGE 3 | André du Bouchet (1924–2001), a French poet and a close friend of Jaccottet. See Jaccottet's *Truinas, 21 April 2001* (John Taylor trans., Les Brouzils, France: The Fortnightly Review, 2018), a tribute to his friend and a meditation on his funeral.

The German soldier's letter may be found in *Lettres de Stalingrad* (Charles Billy trans., Paris: Éditions Buchet-Chastel, 1957).

PAGE 4 | Jaccottet is quoting from Friedrich Hölderlin's *Oeuvres* (Paris: Gallimard-Pléiade, 1967). The Latin phrase means 'I am human, and nothing human is alien to me' and is from *Heauton Timorumenos* (163 BC) by Terence (195/185 – c.159 BC).

PAGE 6 | Henri-Georges Clouzot's film *Les Diaboliques* (1955) was released in the United States as *Diabolique*.

PAGE 8 | Cala Ratjada. Jaccottet stayed for three months (end April–July 1958) in Cala Ratjada, Majorca, thanks to a grant provided by Pro Helvetia.

PAGE 9 | 'You took a lamp and opened the door, / What can be done with a lamp, it's raining, and the sun is rising'— Yves Bonnefoy, *Du movement et de l'immobilité de Douve* (On the Movement and the Immobility of Douve, Paris: Mercure de France, 1953).

'Andromaque, I'm thinking of you . . .' From Charles Baudelaire, 'The Swan' in *Flowers of Evil* (1857).

PAGE 10 | Homer, *The Odyssey*, Volume 2, Book XIII: 28–30: 'But Odysseus would ever turn his head toward the blazing sun, eager to see it, for verily he was eager to return home.' Homer, *The Odyssey* (A. T. Murray trans., Cambridge, MA: Heinemann and Harvard University Press, Loeb Classical Library, 1966).

PAGE 12 | *The Stranger* (1942), by Albert Camus (1913–60), is set under the stark sun of Algeria. By mentioning Camus, alongside the novelists François Mauriac (1885–1970) and André Gide (1869–1951), both of whom are noted for their classical prose styles, Jaccottet is raising an issue that will haunt him throughout his writing life: To what extent does the pursuit of 'style' distance a poet or a writer from 'truth'? Here he contrasts their styles to the poetry of Paul Claudel (1868–1955).

'The familiar empire of future darkness'. Baudelaire, 'Gypsies on the Road' in *Flowers of Evil* (1857).

PAGE 13 | 'This quiet roof, where the doves walk'. The opening line of Paul Valéry's most famous poem, 'The Seaside Cemetery' ('Le Cimetière marin', *Poésies* [Paris: Gallimard, 1933]), set at the cemetery overlooking the Mediterranean at Sète.

The poet Saint-John Perse (1887–1975) is noted for his verse evoking the ocean. Jaccottet has lived in the village of Grignan, in the Drôme area of France, since October 1953.

PAGE 14 | John Cowper Powys, *Les Sables de la mer* (Paris: Plon, 1958). The original novel was published in the US as *Weymouth Sands* (1934) and in the UK as *Jobber Skald* (1935). In the Overlook Press edition (1999) of this novel, see pp. 35–6.

PAGE 16 | Anubis, the Greek name of the god—often depicted as a dog or as a man with a dog's head—associated with mummification and afterlife in ancient Egypt.

PAGE 17 | 'But do not attach your heart to this temporary shelter'. In 'Blazon in Green and White', in *Notebook of*

Greenery (see *And, Nonetheless: Selected Prose and Poetry 1990–2009* [John Taylor trans., New York: Chelsea Editions, 2011]), Jaccottet adds parenthetically: '("But do not attach your heart to this temporary shelter," the courtesan advises the monk in *The Lady of Eguchi*, a Noh play that I read at the age of sixteen and have never forgotten. What if, on the contrary, you never want to detach yourself from it?)'.

PAGE 18 | 'Listen to me . . .'. Jaccottet finds this passage by Meister Eckhart (1260–1328), German theologian and mystical philosopher, in Rudolf Otto's *Le Sacré* (Lausanne: Payot, 1949), p. 27. See also p. 77.

PAGE 20 | Gabriel Bounoure (1886–1969), French critic particularly read and admired by poets of Jaccottet's generation. See his *Marelles sur le parvis* (Paris: Plon, 1958).

PAGE 22 | *A Walk under the Trees* was originally published in French as *La Promenade sous les arbres* (Lausanne: Mermod, 1957).

PAGE 23 | 'The horses stood near the chariots . . .'. Adapted from Homer, *The Iliad*, Volume 1, Book VIII: 564–5 (A. T. Murray trans., Cambridge, MA: Heinemann and Harvard University Press, Loeb Classical Library, 1971). The previous quotation ('the shepherd feels his heart. . .') is adapted from the same translation, line 559.

PAGE 29 | 'Must one speak of God, Truth, Reality? . . .'. Jean Paulhan, *La Nouvelle NRF* (June 1958). Paulhan's *Le Clair et l'Obscur* (Cognac: Le Temps Qu'il Fait, 1983) was prefaced by Jaccottet.

PAGE 31 | 'Through the window of the family home, in L. . . .' In 1933, when Jaccottet was eight, the family moved from Moudon, where he was born, to Lausanne.

PAGE 34 | 'And unto the angel of the church of the Laodiceans write'—Revelation 3:14.

'And unto the angel of the church in Smyrna write'—Revelation 2:8.

'And to the angel of the church in Pergamos write'—Revelation 2:12.

Roud's book *Feuillets* was published by Mermod in 1929.

PAGE 35 | 'We thought we were hearing that nameless bird . . .' Marcel Arland uses these words, by Chateaubriand, as an epigraph for *La Consolation du voyageur* (Paris: Gallimard, 1952).

Jaccottet evokes Jules Verne's novel *Michel Strogoff* in the title text of his book *À partir du mot Russie* (Saint Clément de Rivière: Fata Morgana, 2002), including the captions 'He came to take a breath of air on the wide balcony . . .' and 'There was movement, excitement . . .'.

For the English translation of *Beginning with the Word 'Russia'*, see *A Calm Fire and other Travel Writings* (John Taylor trans., London: Seagull Books, 2019).

The Hetzel edition of Verne's novels remains famous in France. For *Michel Strogoff* (1876), the drawings were made by Jules Frérat and engraved by Charles Barbant.

PAGE 37 | Camille Flammarion's *L'Astronomie populaire* (1880) was a well-known book, with numerous charts and engravings, which summed up what was known of the universe in his day.

'Thus I was speaking . . .' Jaccottet uses this passage from Hölderlin's 'Patmos' (written in 1803, first published in 1808) as a sort of introductory poem in *Un calme feu* (Saint Clément de Rivière: Fata Morgana, 2007). For the English translation of the latter, see *A Calm Fire*. For my translation of this passage, I have returned to the German in Hölderlin's *Sämtliche Gedichte* (Jochen Schmidt ed., Deutscher Klassiker Verlag, 2005). In his notes, Jaccottet cites the Gallimard-Pléiade edition, pp. 867ff.

The painting by Hieronymus Bosch (*c.*1450–1516) referred to here is *Saint John on the Island of Patmos* (1485), found in the Gemäldegalerie (Berlin).

PAGE 39 | 'linked to the star Wormwood that flooded the earth . . .' In French, the same star is called 'Absinthe'. Revelation 8:11: 'And the name of the star is called Wormwood: and the third part of the waters became wormwood; and many men died of the waters, because they were made bitter.'

PAGES 39–40 | 'And he that talked with me had a golden reed to measure the city, and the gates thereof, and the wall thereof'—Revelation 21:15.

'And he shewed me a pure river of water of life, clear as crystal, proceeding out of the throne of God and of the Lamb'—Revelation 22:1.

PAGE 41 | 'the quest that dazzled Neptune . . .'. Jaccottet cites Jacqueline Risset's translation of Dante's *Paradiso*, Canto XXXIII, v. 94–96 (Paris: Flammarion, 1990). The Italian lines read: 'Un punto solo m'è maggior letargo / che venticinque secoli alla impresa / che fe' Nettuno ammirar l'ombra d'Argo.' In her French translation, Risset interprets 'letargo' as 'oubli', and I am following her here by using 'oblivion', not 'lethargy' or 'torpor'.

PAGE 43 | The initials 'A. d. B.' refer to the poet André du Bouchet.

PAGE 44 | 'Words effacing thought . . .' H. L. M. Henry-Louis Mermod (1891–1962), the Swiss publisher for whom Jaccottet worked. This poem is Jaccottet's New Year's Day greetings to Mermod.

PAGE 45 | 'Go by . . .' Maybe his New Year's Day greetings to Swiss photographer Henriette Grindat (1923–1986).

PAGES 45–6 | R. H. Blyth, *Haiku* (4 volumes, Hokusaido Press [undated]). The haikus translated by Jaccottet are in Volume 4, pp. 60, 64, 108, 122, 172, 184, 259.

PAGE 47 | Hölderlin's *The Death of Empedocles* is an unfinished drama, posthumously published in 1846. The play stages the last days of the Greek pre-Socratic philosopher.

L'Obscurité (Gallimard, 1961), Jaccottet's only published novel, recounts the final days of a brilliant philosopher, who is the narrator's mentor. It has been translated into English by Tess Lewis: *Obscurity* (London: Seagull Books, 2015).

PAGE 55 | Plutarch, *La Vie des hommes illustres, Volume 1* (J. Amyot trans., Paris: Gallimard-Pléiade, 1951).

PAGE 62 | Ludwig Tieck (1773–1853), German writer and one of the founding fathers of German Romanticism. Jaccottet refers to Tieck's *Volksmärchen von Peter Lebrecht*, three volumes of plays, stories and fairy tales (1797).

E. T. A. Hoffmann (1776–1822) and Jean Paul (1763–1825), important German Romantic writers.

PAGES 62–3 | 'Patience and time as it goes slowly by.' La Fontaine, 'Le Lion et le Rat' (Book II, Fable 11). In French: 'Patience et longueur de temps'.

PAGE 63 | Alain Borne (1915–62), French poet, killed in a car accident near Avignon.

PAGE 65 | Jaccottet's *Airs* was first published by Gallimard in 1967.

Jaccottet evokes Roud's words in the speech ('Le Combat inégal') he gave when accepting the Schiller Prize in 2010.

PAGE 68 | The death of Jaccottet's father-in-law, Louis Haesler, is evoked in his poetic sequence *Leçons* (Lessons, 1969). It has been translated into English, by Mark Treharne: *Learning* . . . (Birmingham, UK: Delos Press, 2001).

PAGE 74 | *Requiem* was published in 1947.

PAGE 76 | Michel Deguy (b. 1930), French poet who has translated works by Martin Heidegger.

'I have reached the middle of my age . . .' An allusion to the first line of Dante's *Inferno*.

PAGE 78 | For Plato, Jaccottet is quoting from the *Oeuvres completes*, *Volume 3* (Cambry, Garnier trans., no date). The English translation is from *The Dialogues of Plato*, *Volume 1*, (B. Jowett trans., New York: Random House, 1892), p. 499.

PAGE 80 | *Connaissance de l'Est* (1900) is a collection of poems by Paul Claudel which he wrote mostly in China between 1895 and 1899. The book has been translated into English as *The East I Know*. Jaccottet alludes here to Claudel's poetic prose text 'La Maison suspendue'.

The *NRF* (*La Nouvelle Revue française*) is the famous literary review founded by Gallimard in 1909. Many of Jaccottet's articles and poems have appeared in it over the decades.

PAGE 81 | 'Time, a child playing'—from one of Heraclitus' fragments. The pre-Socratic Greek philosopher adds: 'playing at draughts' or 'at a board game'.

PAGE 82 | The French poet René Char (1907–88) wrote his text on a poster he made in 1959, when the first Russian sputniks were launched.

The Italian poet and philosopher Giacomo Leopardi (1798–1837) juxtaposed the infinity of desire and the finitude of pleasure. Only illusion, notably through poetry, could give the impression that the gap had been bridged. Jaccottet often quotes from and analyses Leopardi's poems and prose writings.

PAGE 83 | Giuseppe Ungaretti, *Innocence et mémoire* (Paris: Gallimard, 1969), pp. 359–61. Jaccottet was the French translator of Ungaretti (1888–1970). See their *Correspondence (1946–1970)* (José-Flore Tappy ed.) (Paris: Gallimard, 2008).

PAGE 84 | Through his translations, notably of *The Man without Qualities* (1930–43), Jaccottet introduced French readers to the work of Robert Musil (1880–1942).

PAGE 91 | Books by Russian philosopher Léon Shestov (1866–1938) were often read by French poets in Jaccottet's generation; several have now been reprinted by Éditions Le Bruit du temps, including *Sur la balance de Job* (1929).

PAGE 92 | Piero Sadun (1919–74), Italian artist who was born and lived in Sienna.

PAGE 94 | Clairvaux Prison. On 21 September 1971, two convicts, Claude Buffet and Roger Bontems, took a nurse, Nicole Comte, and a prison guard, Guy Girardot, as hostages in an attempt to escape. Buffet murdered them during the assault of the police the next day. Both convicts were captured, put on trial, given the death sentence and guillotined.

PAGE 95 | Honoré de Balzac (1799–1850) published his novel *Cousin Pons* in 1847. It is the story of a good and naive man who becomes a victim.

PAGE 99 | Roger Martin du Gard (1881–1958), French novelist. His novel *Le lieutenant-colonel de Maumort*, on which he worked between 1941 and 1958, was published posthumously in 1983.

Jacques Copeau (1879–1949), French drama critic, playwright and founder of Théâtre du Vieux-Colombier.

André Gide (1869–1951), French novelist whose flat on the rue Vaneau (in the seventh arrondissement), where he lived from 1926 to his death, is well known because of the numerous writers who paid him visits there.

Gide's *Les Caves du Vatican* (1914), which has appeared in English as *The Vatican Cellars*, has also been translated as *Lafcadio's Adventures*.

PAGE 105 | Father Huc—Évariste Régis Huc (1813–1860), French Catholic missionary and travel writer. His book *Souvenirs d'un voyage dans la Tartarie, le Thibet, et la Chine pendant les années 1844, 1845 et 1846* appeared in Paris in 1850 and was very popular.

PAGE 106 | Jacques Borel, *La Dépossession* (Paris: Gallimard, 1973). Borel (1925–2002) was a French novelist and this book is the diary he kept while his mother was staying in the Ligenère Psychiatric Hospital.

Claude Mauriac (1914–96), Bertrand Poirot-Delpech (1929–2006) and Michel Cournot (1922–2007), all notable book reviewers at the time.

PAGE 107 | Jude Stéfan (b. 1930), French poet and short-story writer. Jean Tortel (1904–93), French poet.

PAGE 108 | 'Thinking of the piece of writing that I am working on . . .' In a footnote dated 2008, Jaccottet writes: '*Chants d'en bas*, perhaps; or *À travers un verger?*' *Chants d'en bas* (Songs from Below) was first published in 1974 by Payot. In English, it is included in *Selected Poems* (Derek Mahon trans., Winston-Salem, NC: Wake Forest University Press, 1988). *À travers un verger* (Through an Orchard) was first published in 1973 by Fata Morgana. In English, it was rendered as *Through an Orchard* (Mark Treharne trans., *Prospice* 9 [1978]).

Pierre Leyris (1907–2001), editor, at Mercure de France (where the series 'Domaine anglais' is published), and prolific translator of English literature (Shakespeare, Blake, Melville, Eliot, Yeats, Dickens, Stevenson, Milton, Hawthorne, among many others).

PAGES 108–09 | Louis-Ferdinand Céline (1894–1961), considered among the first twentieth-century French novelists to introduce slang and colloquial terms and syntax into his literary language.

Jean Giono (1895–1970), French novelist known for his novels evoking simple farmers in the south of France.

The writers Julien Gracq (1910–2007) and André Pieyre de Mandiargues (1909–91), associated with the surrealist movement and considered to wield especially elegant, highly personal writing styles.

André Dhôtel (1900–91), novelist and close to Jaccottet in several ways: see their correspondence and Jaccottet's essays in *Avec André Dhôtel* (Saint Clément de Rivière: Fata Morgana, 2008).

Marcel Arland (1899–1986), novelist, literary critic and editor.

Henri Thomas (1912–93), not only a novelist but also a translator of German and English-language literature; close to Jaccottet. See their correspondence, *Pépiement des ombres* (Philippe Blanc ed., Saint Clément de Rivière: Fata Morgana, 2018).

PAGE 109 | Jaccottet refers to Pierre Madaule's *Une tâche sérieuse?* (Paris: Gallimard, 1973). See *Correspondence 1953–2002* (Gallimard, 2012) between Madaule and Blanchot.

Jacques Madaule (1898-1993), Catholic intellectual and writer and Pierre Madaule's father.

PAGE 110 | Rudolf Kassner (1873–1959), Czech writer and philosopher; close friend of Rainer Maria Rilke. Rilke's eighth 'Duino Elegy' is dedicated to him.

Christiane Martin du Gard (1907–73), Roger Martin du Gard's daughter. Appointed Jaccottet to be her literary executor, a role that explains some of the allusions in this passage.

Wayland Dobson, a harpsichord maker who died in 2000 at the age of 81. Mentioned in the sequence *Ce peu de bruits*. (See 'These Slight Noises' in *And, Nonetheless*).

Château du Tertre—Roger Martin du Gard's residence during the years 1925–58 and now home to his museum.

PAGE 112 | André Frénaud (1907–93) and Jean Tardieu (1903–95), French poets.

Jean Hélion (1904–87), French artist.

Georges Auclair (1920–2014) and Henri Petit (1900–78), French writers.

André Berne-Joffroy (1915–2007), French critic and art curator. He appears in Jaccottet's *Truinas, 21 April 2001*.

PAGE 113 | Pierre Herbart (1903–74), French writer. See Jean-Luc Moreau's biography *Pierre Herbart, l'orgueil du dépouillement* (Paris: Grasset, 2014).

Fernand Dubuis (1908–91), Swiss painter who lived at the Château du Tertre, beginning in 1961.

PAGE 114 | In Greek mythology, the Atreidae are the descendants of Atreus and are noted for murder, parricides, infanticides and incest.

PAGE 115 | *Judith* by Jean Giraudoux (1882–1944) was first published in 1931.

Claudel published his *Conversations dans le Loir-et-Cher* in 1935.

Silvia Monfort (1923–1991), actress, stage director and novelist.

The sixteenth arrondissement is proverbially one of the ritziest of Paris.

Poet, writer and translator Valery Larbaud (1881–1957) published *Allen* in 1927, a long story consisting almost entirely of dialogue.

PAGE 116 | Both 'The Beast in the Jungle' (1903) and 'The Altar of the Dead' (1895) are stories by Henry James (1843–1916).

Louis Soutter (1871–1942), Swiss artist. In a footnote, Jaccottet adds: 'The excellent Vaudois painter Charles Chinet [1871–1978]'.

PAGE 120 | Jaccottet's aforementioned *Chants d'en bas* ('Songs from Below') appeared in August 1974.

PAGE 122 | In the Authurian legends, King Mark of Cornwall is the uncle of Tristan and the husband of Isolde.

PAGE 123 | Simone Girard (1898–1985) organized concerts for the Société de Musique de Chambre d'Avignon (Société Avignonnaise de Concerts).

PAGE 125 | *Ruines avec figures* by Franco Lucentini (1920–2002), a collection of short stories translated by Jaccottet in 1975. In Italian: *Notiᵹie degli scavi* (1973).

PAGE 126 | *The Sunday Woman*—the novel by Franco Lucentini and Carlo Fruttero (1926–2012), published in 1972 and made into a film, directed by Luigi Comencini, in 1975. Jaccottet translated it as *La Femme du dimanche* (1973). In Italian: *La donna della domenica* (1972).

Jaccottet had already translated Marc Chagall's poems (*Poèmes*, Geneva: Cramer, 1968). A second edition appeared in 1975.

PAGE 129 | Lamberto Vitali (1896–1992), Italian art critic, and a close friend and specialist of the artist Giorgio Morandi. Jaccottet writes about Morandi in *The Pilgrim's Bowl* (John Taylor trans., London: Seagull Books, 2015).

About Paul Celan's translations of Mandelstam, Jaccottet notes: 'Translations that appeared in 1954. I no longer remember when I had read them.' Celan's many translations of Mandelstam can be found in *Gesammelte Werke, Volume 5, Übertragungen II* (Frankfurt: Suhrkamp, 2000).

Ivar Ivask (1927–92), Estonian poet and literary scholar. From 1967 to 1991, editor-in-chief of *World Literature Today*. His wife was the Latvian poet and translator Astrid Ivask (1926–2015).

PAGE 131 | René Char, *Le Nu perdu* (Paris: Gallimard, 1971). In Char's *Selected Poems* (New York: New Directions, 1992) and *Furor and Mystery & Other Writings* (Boston,

MA: Black Widow Press, 2010), this title was translated as *Nakedness Lost*.

Yves Bonnefoy (1923–2016). *Dans le leurre du seuil* (Paris: Mercure de France, 1975). The poems in Bonnefoy's book have been translated variously under the titles 'The Lure of the Threshold' and 'In the Threshold's Lure'. See, most recently, *Poems of Yves Bonnefoy* (Manchester: Carcanet, 2017).

Yves Bonnefoy, *Hier régnant desert* (Paris: Mercure de France, 1958). Anthony Rudolf has translated it as *Yesterday's Wilderness Kingdom* (London: Modern Poets in Translation Books, 2000).

Jean-Claude Renard (1922–2002) was a French poet.

PAGE 132 | Jaccottet is thinking of Larbaud's *Jaune Bleu Blanc* (1927). Made up of notes, prose texts, and short fictions, the book was described by its author as: 'A yellow, light blue, and white ribbon was long used as a way of tying together the manuscripts that now form this book.'

PAGE 133 | Saint-John Perse (1887–1975), French poet and diplomat.

In French: *La Semaison*, pp. 223–4. The page 268 cited in the text corresponds to the Seagull Books translation by Tess Lewis (*Seedtime*, 2013).

The poem by Mandelstam analysed here is the one with the line 'I was washing myself at night in the yard.'

PAGE 135 | Jaccottet's relationship to Francis Ponge (1899–1988) was important in his coming of age as a writer. See Jaccottet's *Ponge, Pâturages, Prairies* (Paris: Le Bruit du Temps, 2015). The 'ripostes' are against Marcelin Pleynet (b. 1933), poet and art critic who was the director of the review *Tel Quel* between 1962 and 1982, and the poet Christian Prigent (b. 1945), who wrote his doctoral thesis about Ponge. The dispute with Pleynet arose because of Ponge's disapproval of the former's Maoist-oriented political stance.

Michel Debré (1912–1996), important Gaullist political figure in France.

PAGE 136 | Henri Maldiney (1912–2013), philosopher and critic who wrote an essential book about Ponge's work, *Le Legs des choses dans l'oeuvre de Francis Ponge* (Lausanne: L'Âge d'homme, 1974). Ponge refers to Jaccottet's piece in the *Nouvelle Revue française* (July 1974).

Jaccottet translated poems by Góngora in *Les Solitudes* (Geneva: La Dogana, 1984) and *Treize sonnets et un fragment* (Geneva: La Dogana, 1985).

Claude Garache (b. 1930), French painter and a close friend of Jaccottet.

PAGE 139 | René Étiemble (1909–2002), university professor known for his work in Chinese literature.

Bernard Pivot (b. 1935) hosted the television literary talk show *Apostrophe*s between 1974 and 1990, and then *Bouillon de cultur*e between 1991 and 2001.

Jacques Chardonne (1884–1968), collaborationist and extreme-right-wing writer, sometimes still admired for his work; Mitterrand notably expressed his admiration for Chardonne's *oeuvr*e.

PAGE 140 | Jules Supervielle (1884–1960), French poet born in Uruguay.

Denis de Rougemont (1906–85), Swiss university professor and essayist.

Jaccottet refers to Michel Leiris's *Journal de Chine*, eventually published by Gallimard in 1994, which recounts a trip taken in 1955.

PAGE 141 | The Swiss writer Adolf Muschg (b. 1934) published *Goethe als Emigrant* in 1986.

The Austrian writer Peter Handke (b. 1942) indeed refers often to Goethe in his various notebooks.

PAGE 142 | Francis Ponge and Jean Paulhan, *Correspondance (1923–1968)* (Paris: Gallimard, 1986). Paulhan (1884–1968) was a writer and a key editor at Gallimard.

Jean Tardieu's witty *Le Professeur Froeppel* was first published by Gallimard in 1978.

Michel Lonsdale (b. 1931), French actor who often recites from or interprets literary works.

Claude Mauriac, son of novelist François Mauriac, was associated with the French New Novel in its initial period.

PAGE 143 | Jaccottet refers to his poem in *L'Effraie* (The Barn-Owl, 1953), which forms the ninth part of the sequence 'La Semaison: Notes pour des poèmes' and begins 'Le fleuve craquelé se trouble' ('The crackled river becomes muddy').

The Italian composer Giacinto Scelsi (1905–88). The Belgian poet and writer Henri Michaux (1899–1984). See Jaccottet's *A Calm Fire* for other evocations of Scelsi.

The original French title of the long poem by poet François de Malherbe (1555–1628) is 'Les Larmes de saint Pierre' (1587). Ponge's book about Malherbe is *Pour un Malherbe* (Paris: Gallimard, 1977).

PAGE 144 | Goethe's poem 'Zueignung' is the 'dedication' at the beginning of *Faust*.

PAGE 145 | Canadian pianist Glenn Gould (1932–82). Jaccottet is an avid listener to classical and especially baroque music, and himself plays the harpsichord. The harpsichord in his house in Grignan was built by Wayland Dobson.

PAGE 146 | Pierre Dumayet (1923–2011), writer, journalist and television moderator; his television series *Lectures pour tous* (1953–68) was the first French literary talk show. Jaccottet is thus comparing it to Pivot's *Apostrophes* series.

Paulhan wrote a book about the art of Jean Fautrier (1898–1964), *Fautrier l'enragé* (Paris: Gallimard, 1962). For the Paulhan–Ungaretti correspondence, see *Correspondance (1921–1968)* (Paris: Gallimard, 1989).

PAGE 148 | Umberto Saba (1883–1957), Italian poet. Jaccottet refers here to *Du 'Canzoniere'*, as translated into French by Philippe Renard and Bernard Simeone (Paris: La Différence, 1992). My translation. See also *Songbook: Selected Poems* (Stephen Sartarelli trans., Rhinebeck, NY: The Sheep Meadow Press, 1998) and *Poetry and Prose* (Vincent Moleta trans., Bridgetown: Aeolian Press, 2004).

Jan Skácel (1922–89), Czech poet. Eight poems by Skácel are translated by Jaccottet in *D'un lyre à cinq cordes* (Paris: Gallimard, 1997).

PAGES 148–9 | John Keats (1795–1821) wrote 'Ode to a Nightingale' in 1819. Jaccottet refers to the well-known 'Orphée' paperback volumes of world poetry published by Éditions La Différence.

PAGE 149 | Swiss poet Pierre-Louis Matthey (1893–1970), author of *Seize à Vingt* (1914), was also a translator of English-language poetry. Jaccottet is referring to Matthey's translation in *Tendre est la nuit* (Lausanne: Mermod, 1950).

Une transaction secrète (Paris: Gallimard, 1987) gathers Jaccottet's essays about translation and translated poetry. He adds in a footnote: 'Today, in 2009, I fortunately have Bonnefoy's version.' Bonnefoy's version can be found in his *Keats et Leopardi* (Paris: Mercure de France, 2000).

The book-length poem *Le Requiem* (1962) by Jean Cocteau (1889-1963) was published by Gallimard in 1962.

Olivier Larronde (1927–65) was a poet.

'Singbarer Rest', the first words of a poem in Paul Celan's *Atemwende* (1967).

PAGE 150 | The Swiss writer Robert Walser (1878–1956). The title in German is *Geschwister Tanner* (1907). Jaccottet refers to the French translation *Les Enfants Tanner* (Jean Launay trans., Paris: Gallimard, 1985).

Henri Thomas' *Le Goût de l'éternel* was published by Gallimard in 1990.

Panorama refers to a literary noontime programme (1968–1999) on the national radio station France Culture, where critics discussed recent books.

The page number given here corresponds to Tess Lewis' translation: *The Second Seedtime*. In the French edition: *La Seconde Semaison*, p. 133.

For the Spanish playwright Pedro Calderón de la Barca (1600–81), Jaccottet refers to *Le Prince constant*, as translated by Bernard Sesé and published by Aubier in 1989. The original Spanish play, *El príncipe constante*, dates to 1629.

PAGE 151 | Bashō's book has also been translated as *The Narrow Road to the Interior*. Written in prose and verse, it is a travel diary of a dangerous trip, made on foot by the poet (1644–94), through seventeenth-century Edo Japan. Jaccottet has himself translated many Japanese haiku poems; see *Haïku* (Saint Clément de Rivière: Fata Morgana, 2010).

PAGES 151–2| *Cahier de verdure* was published by Gallimard in 1990. The book is entirely translated as *Notebook of Greenery* in *And, Nonetheless*.

PAGE 155 | For Shestov, Jaccottet refers to *Athènes et Jérusalem* (B. de Schloezer trans., Paris: Flammarion, 1967), reprinted: 2011, Le Bruit du temps. In English: *Athens and Jerusalem* (Bernard Martin trans., Athens: Ohio University Press, 1966).

17 January 1991—the day that Iraq fired eight Scud missiles on Israel and the US–led coalition forces began the Desert Storm campaign by bombing Iraq.

PAGES 156–7 | Goethe, *Iphigenia in Taurus* (1779). A reworking of Euripides' play *Iphigenia in Taurus* or *Iphigenia among the Taurians* (414–412 BC).

Goethe, *West-östlicher Divan* (1819–27), 'Lied und Gebilde' in *Buch des Sängers*. Translated into English as *West-East Divan*. In a footnote, for the German verses quoted, Jaccottet offers this French equivalent, which he qualifies as 'badly translated': 'Le feu de l'âme ainsi éteint, / En chanson retentira; / Par un poète à la main pure / Puisée, l'eau s'arrondira.'

PAGE 158 | Henri Thomas, *Ai-je une patrie?* (Paris: Gallimard, 1991).

PAGE 159 | The German title of Goethe and Schiller's review was *Die Propyläen* (1798–1800).

PAGE 160 | The original French novel by Pascal Quignard (b. 1948) is *Tous les matins du monde* (Paris: Gallimard, 1992). In English: *All the World's Mornings* (James Kirkup trans., Minneapolis, MN: Graywolf Press, 1993).

PAGES 161–2 | Among the poets mentioned in the context of this visit to Jean Tortel (1904–93): Henri Deluy (b. 1931), Gérard Arseguel (b. 1938), Jean-Jacques Viton (b. 1933), Liliane Giraudon (b. 1946) and Claude Royet-Journoud (b. 1941) can roughly be classified in the 'linguistically experimental' category of contemporary French poetry, whereas Paul de Roux (1937–2016) and Jean-Pierre Lemaire (b. 1948) are much closer to Jaccottet's poetic sensibility.

PAGE 162 | The poet Tristan L'Hermite (1601–55) was active in the baroque period preceding that in which Jean-Philippe Rameau (1683–1764) composed his pieces for the harpsichord.

Tortel was one of the main contributors to the review *Cahiers du Sud* (1925–1966).

PAGE 164 | Jaccottet has translated Ungaretti's last poem, 'L'impietrito e il velluto', in *Anthologie bilingue de la poésie italienne* (Paris: Gallimard-Pléiade, 1974), p. 1334, as well as in *Vie d'un homme* (Paris: Éditions de Minuit/Gallimard, Collection Poésie, 198), p. 328.

PAGES 164–5 | Marcel Proust, *Jean Santeuil* (begun in 1895, published only in 1952). Jaccottet notes that this comes from the Gallimard-Pléiade volume (1971) of *Jean Santeuil*, p. 520.

Anna de Noailles (1876–1933), French poetess of Romanian origin.

PAGE 166 | Carl Larsson (1853–1919), Swedish painter.

At the Vasa Museum, Jaccottet is looking at the 64-gun warship that sunk on its maiden voyage in 1628 and was salvaged.

PAGE 168 | Jacques Audiberti, *Lettres à Jean Paulhan (1933–1965)* (Paris: Gallimard, 1993). Audiberti (1899–1965) was a writer, poet and playwright.

Toujours (1943) is now available in a Gallimard paperback volume titled *Des tonnes de semences / Toujours / La Nouvelle origine* (1981).

Jaccottet's father was a veterinarian.

PAGE 170 | Christian Zacharias (b. 1950), German pianist and conductor.

PAGE 171 | Lélo Fiaux, *Journal d'un peintre* (Lausanne: La Bibliothèque des Arts, 1994).

Gabriel Pomerand (1925–72), poet and one of the founders of Lettrism, a movement established in the mid-1940s by Romanian writer, poet and artist Isidore Isou (1925–2007).

PAGE 172 | For Bobrahim Mashrab (1653–1711), Jaccottet is reading *La Vagabond flamboyant* (Paris: Gallimard, 1993). Mashrab was a major figure of Sufi poetry and, specifically, of Uzbek poetry.

PAGE 173 | For the passage on Plato's *Republic*, the page number cited corresponds to Tess Lewis' translation, *The Second Seedtime*. For the original French, *La Second semaison*, see p. 204. The myth of Er is found at the end of *The Republic* (10.614–10.621): 'There came also the soul of Odysseus having yet to make a choice, and his lot happened to be the last of them all. Now the recollection of former toils had disenchanted him of ambition, and he went about for a considerable time in search of the life of a private man who had no cares; he had some difficulty in finding this, which was lying about and had been neglected by everybody else; and when he saw it, he said that he would have done the same had his lot been first instead of last, and that he was delighted to have it.' *The Dialogues of Plato, Volume 1* (B. Jowett trans., New York: Random House, 1937), p. 878.

PAGE 174 | For the fragment 'Columbus' in French, see Hölderlin, *Oeuvres*, p. 1226. Jaccottet also quotes this fragment in his tribute to André du Bouchet, *Truinas, 21 April 2001*.

PAGES 174–5 | The fragment is from Mallarmé's 'Autre éventail de Mademoiselle Mallarmé'.

PAGE 178 | Jaccottet refers to the French edition of Bertolucci's *La Chambre* (M. Gallet trans., Lagrasse: Verdier, 1988). In English, see *The Bedroom* (Luigi Bonaffini trans., New York: Chelsea Editions, 2012).

Jaccottet's *Autres journées* was published by Fata Morgana in 1987.

See *The Pilgrim's Bowl* for Jaccottet's discussion of Morandi's reading of Pascal and Leopardi.

PAGE 179 | Temple Solaire sect. The Ordre du temple solaire was founded in Geneva in 1984. Jaccottet specifically refers to the collective suicide, in Switzerland, of 48 members of the sect on 4 October 1994.

PAGE 180–1 | Yves Bonnefoy, *Rome, 1630* (Paris: Flammarion, 1993). In English: see Hoyt Rogers' translation (*Rome, 1630: The Horizon of the Early Baroque*, London: Seagull Books, 2020).

The State of Things (*Der Stand der Dinge*) by Wim Wenders, was first shown in 1982. Michelangelo Antonioni's *Red Desert* (*Il desserto rosso*) is from 1964. Federico Fellini's *La Dolce Vita*, 1960.

For Bonnefoy's analysis of Morandi's art, see *Le Nuage rouge* (Paris: Gallimard-Folio, 1999) and *Remarques sur le regard—Picasso / Giacometti / Morandi* (Paris: Calman-Levy, 2002).

PAGE 182 | Joseph Joubert (1754–1824), French writer known for the aphorisms and short philosophical texts of his *Carnets* (two volumes, Paris: Gallimard, 1994). In the French edition of *La Seconde Semaison*, see pp. 224–5. In the English translation by Tess Lewis, see pp. 244–5.

PAGE 183 | Paul Valéry, *Ego scriptor* (Paris: Poésie-Gallimard, 1992), pp. 29–30.

George Steiner, *Martin Heidegger* (Paris: Flammarion, 1981). In English: *Heidegger* (London: Fontana, 1978), p. 69.

PAGE 185 | Dante, *L'Enfer* (J. Risset trans., Paris: Flammarion, 1985). *Inferno*, Canto XXXII, lines 23–4. Jaccottet uses Dante's imagery of Hell when he refers to Kolyma in the 'Darkness and Cold, Here is Hell . . .' chapter of *A Calm Fire*. The final quoted passage is from *Inferno*, Canto XXXIV, lines 127–34. The translations here are from Mark Musa's version (London: Penguin, 2003).

PAGE 188 | Lionel Jospin (b. 1937), French politician. A member of the Socialist Party, he has held several high-level positions, including that of prime minister (1997–2002). At the time of Jaccottet's dream, Jospin, the Socialist Party presidential candidate, had just been beaten, on 23 April

1995, during the first round of the election, by right-wing candidate Jacques Chirac and extreme right-wing candidate Jean-Marie Le Pen; he thus could not accede to the second round (won by Chirac). Until a few days before the election, all polls showed that Jospin would attain the second round. The fact that Le Pen obtained more votes than Jospin in the first round was experienced as a trauma by the vast majority of French voters.

PAGES 189–90 | Baudelaire's poem, which in French begins 'La servante au grand cœur dont vous étiez jalouse', has been translated here by Francis Scarfe (*Baudelaire: The Complete Poems*, London: Anvil Press, 2012). It is included in *Les Fleurs du mal* (The Flowers of Evil, 1861).

Pierre Delisle (1908–2000), poet who published some of his work in *Cahiers du Sud*. Jaccottet wrote about his poetry in *L'Entretien des muses* (Paris: Gallimard, 1968).

PAGE 193 | Friedhelm Kemp (1914–2011), translated several books by Jaccottet into German.

Christine Lavant (1915–1973), Austian poet. In English, her poetry can be read in *Shatter the Bell in My Ear* (David Chorlton trans., Fayetteville, NY: Bitter Oleander Press, 2017).

Henri Meschonnic, *Les Cinq Rouleaux* (Paris: Gallimard, 1970). Meschonnic (1932–2009) was a poet, linguist, and translator (notably, of the Bible).

PAGE 196 | 'Visit to Truinas'—Anne de Staël (b. 1942), daughter of painter Nicolas de Staël (1913–1955); poet and the last wife of André du Bouchet.

PAGE 197 | Julien Green (1900–98), American novelist who wrote in French.

PAGE 199 | Georges Duthuit, *Le Feu des signes* (Geneva: Skira, 1962). Sinan the architect (1488/89–1588) was the main architect for the sultans Suleiman the Magnificent, Selim II and Murad III.

PAGE 200 | *Landscape with Blind Orion Searching for the Sun* (1658) by Nicolas Poussin (1594–1665); Metropolitan Museum, New York.

The Pilgrims of Emmaus (1628) is by Rembrandt (1606–69).

Green and Maroon (1953) by Mark Rothko (1903–70); The Phillips Collection (Washington).

Kafū Nagai (1879–1959), penname of Japanese author Sokichi Nagai.

Nachi Waterfall, a hanging scroll painting from the Kamakura period (thirteenth–fourteenth century); Nezu Art Museum, Tokyo.

PAGE 201 | Hölderin's poem begins:

'Wie wenn am Feiertage, das Feld zu sehn,
Ein Landmann geht, des Morgens, wenn
Aus heißer Nacht die kühlenden Blitze fielen
Die ganze Zeit und fern noch tönet der Donner . . .'

[As when on his day of rest, a farmer goes out
In early morning to see his field, after a whole night
When cooling lightning had fallen out of the stifling
      heat,
And thunder still sounds in the distance . . .]

PAGE 203 | 'vain ornaments'—'Que ces vains ornements, que ces voiles me pèsent!' (Jean Racine, *Phèdre* [1677], I, 3). 'These vain ornaments, these veils, how they weigh down on me!'

PAGE 205 | *Carnets 1995–1998* (*La Semaison, III*), pp. 120–3.

Jacques Borel (1925–2002), writer of oft-autobiographical novels. *L'Effacement* was published by Gallimard in 1998.

The allusion 'green paradise of childhood loves'—from Baudelaire's 'Moesta et errabunda': 'vert paradis des amours enfantines'.

Chardin's *Child with a Teetotum* (1735) is in the Louvre.

Rilke's 'Requiem for a Friend', written in tribute to the artist Paula Modersohn-Becker (1876–1907).

PAGE 206 | CERN, the European Organization for Nuclear Research operates a particle physics research laboratory. The 'ring' here refers to the linear accelerators of the laboratory.

PAGE 207 | 'Michel Houellebecq face à Philippe Sollers, réponse aux "imbéciles"', *Le Nouvel Observateur*, 8 October 1998. Houellebecq (b. 1956) and Sollers (b. 1936) are French novelists.

PAGE 208 | Jaccottet is referring to Russian artist Ilya Kabakov (b. 1933).

Charles Péguy (1873–1914), *Le Porche du mystère de la deuxième vertu* (Paris: Gallimard, 1929).

PAGE 210 | 'To What Serves Mortal Beauty', *The Poems of Gerard Manley Hopkins* (W. H. Gardner and N. H. MacKenzie eds., Oxford: Oxford University Press, 1967), p. 98. Jaccottet uses Leyris's translation of Hopkins' *Poèmes* (Paris: Seuil, 1957).

PAGE 216 | Rimbaud's phrase 'J'ai oublié tout mon devoir humain pour le suivre' is found in the prose text 'Ravings 1, Foolish Virgin, The Infernal Bridegroom', *A Season in Hell* (1873).

Jaccottet refers to the German romantic poet and writer Novalis (1772–1801).

PAGE 219 | 'uomo qualunque', an Italian expression for 'any man', 'ordinary man'.

For a Yes or For a No, play by Nathalie Sarraute (1900–99); in French: *Pour un oui ou pour un non* (Paris: Gallimard, 1982).

Claude Régy (1923–2019), French stage director.

PAGE 220 | Ermolay Lopakhin, one of the main characters of Chekhov's play *The Cherry Orchard*. Uncle Vanya is the main character of the homonymous play.

Pétrarque, *Aux amis, lettres familières (1330–1331)* (Christophe Carraud trans., Grenoble: Éditions Jérôme Millon, 1998).

PAGE 221 | Alvaro Mutis's *Contextos para Maqroll* (Contexts for Maqroll) was published in 1997. Mutis (1923–2013) was a Colombian poet, novelist and essayist.

The *Tropics* by Henry Miller (1891–1980) that Jaccottet refers to are the novels *Tropic of Cancer* (1934) and *Tropic of Capricorn* (1939).

'Arald', former acronym used by the regional association devoted to books and reading: Auvergne-Rhône-Alpes Livre et Lecture.

Patrick Laupin (b. 1950), writer and poet.

PAGE 222 | Jorge Luis Borges, *Fictions* (Paris: Gallimard, 1951).

Simone Weil (1909–43) in *Pensées sans ordre concernant l'amour de Dieux* (Paris: Gallimard, 1962). Republished in *Oeuvres* (Paris: Gallimard-Quarto, 1999).

Joë Bousquet (1897–1950), French writer. Wounded in 1918 during the First World War, he remained paralysed for the rest of his life.

Jean-François Billeter, *Leçons sur Tchouang-tseu* (Paris: Allia, 2002).

PAGE 223 | 'coming back from the Val des Nymphes'. See 'Colours in the Distance' in *And, Nonetheless*, pp. 246–55.

PAGE 228 | *La Cantate à trois voix*, poetic work written in 1911–12 by Paul Claudel.

Paul Valéry's lines 'Midi le juste y compose de feux / La mer, la mer toujours recommence . . .' are from the first strophe of 'Le Cimetière marin' (1920).

PAGE 229 | Goethe, *Briefwechsel mit Zelter*, in *Sämtliche Werke, Volume 20/ 1* (Munich: Hanser, 1998).

Virgile, *Enéide* (Bellessort trans., Paris: Les Belles Lettres, 1938).

PAGE 230 | Felix Mendelssohn (1809–47) met Goethe several times and set some of his poems to music.

PAGES 230–1 | Czeslaw Milosz (1911–2004), Polish poet.

PAGE 231 | Jules Supervielle (1884–1960), *Oeuvres poétiques completes* (Paris: Gallimard-Pléiade, 1996).

PAGE 233 | Alain Finkielkraut (b. 1949), French journalist and philosopher. On his long-standing radio-interview show on the France Culture network, *Répliques*, he hosts writers and academics to debate current issues.

PAGE 234 | Michel Leiris (1901–90). Jaccottet refers to *Haut mal* (Paris: Gallimard, 1943), a polysemous title that is also an expression for 'epilepsy'. In English, three volumes of the four-volume series *The Rules of the Game* were published by the Yale University Press in 2017, in Lydia Davis' translations: *Volume 1: Scratches*; *Volume 2: Scraps*; *Volume 3: Fibrils*.

PAGE 235 | Patrick Ayrton (b. 1961), British harpsichordist and conductor.

André Frénaud, *Les Rois mages* (Paris: Poésie-Gallimard, 1987).

PAGES 235–6 | Robert Marteau, *Liturgie* (Seyssel: Champ Vallon, 1992). Marteau (1925–2011) was a poet and novelist.

PAGES 236–7 | *Anthologie de la poésie allemande* (Paris: Gallimard-Pléiade, p. 260).

Quirinus Kuhlmann (1651–89), German baroque poet and mystic. The title of his autobiographical *Kühlpsalter*, literally 'Cool-Psalter', also puns with his name.

Jaccottet writes at somewhat more length about the sixteenth-century Spanish mystic Saint John of the Cross in his poetic prose texts 'Violets', 'Another Parentheses' and 'Colours in the Distance' as well as in *These Slight Noises* (all included in *And, Nonetheless*). Note that the 'enigmatic mentioning' of the Biblical figure, Aminadab, occurs, not in the poem 'En una noche oscura' but in the *Spiritual Canticle* (strophe 39 in the first version, strophe 40 in the second).

PAGE 238 | Polish poet Adam Zagajewski (b. 1945). Jaccottet refers to *Palissades, marronniers, liseron, Dieu* (Paris: Fayard, 1989). Zagajewski, born in 1945, has been extensively translated into English. The translation here is by Clare Cavanagh and been specially done for this book.

Vladimir Holan (1905–80)—Czech poet. Zbigniew Herbert (1924–98)—Polish poet.

PAGE 239 | André du Bouchet, *Annotations sur l'espace non datées* (*Carnet 3*) (Saint Clément de Rivière: Fata Morgana, 2000).

PAGE 240 | Mozart's *Concerto Jeunehomme* is his Piano Concerto No. 9, composed in 1777 for pianist Louise Victoire Jenamy (1749–1812), the 'Jenamy' having been transformed into 'Jeunehomme'.

Clara Haskil (1895–1960), Romanian and Swiss pianist.

Georg Ludwig Jochum (1909–70), German conductor.

Painter and engraver Gérard de Palézieux (1919–2012), one of the oldest friends of the author. See Jaccottet's *Remarques sur Palézieux* (Saint Clément de Rivière: Fata Morgana, 2005).

Michel and Loukie Rossier were friends of the Jaccottets, who often took trips to Italy in their company. Michel Rossier, a Swiss art collector, music lover and benefactor who owned a marble works in Vevey, gave financial support to numerous writers, musicians and artists. He and his wife organized trips for and with the Jaccottets (to Italy, London, Greece and New York) up to a final one, to Italy, in June 1997. In Jaccottet's tribute to his close friend, he writes: 'Approaching the enigma of flowers is less difficult, probably, than expressing the quality of human beings, since one has scruples about touching upon it with words' (*Un humaniste dans la cite*, Fondation pour les Arts et les Lettres, Vevey, 2002). See *A Calm Fire*.

The 'Anne' evoked here is of course Anne de Staël, the wife of André du Bouchet.

Landscapes with Absent Figures (Mark Treharne trans., London: Menard Press, 1998). Much of *Ce peu de bruits* has been translated as *These Slight Noises* and is included in *And, Nonetheless* but the second part of the original French *Ce peu de bruits*, which includes the text on Senancour, was not translated for this American edition.

Étienne Pivert de Senancour (1770–1846), writer associated with French romanticism.

Jaccottet's *Truinas, 21 April 2001* recalls that a passage from Senancour's *Oberman* (1804) was read at du Bouchet's funeral.

PAGE 243 | Jean-Christophe Bailly, *La Légende dispersée* (Paris: Christian Bourgois, 2001).

PAGE 244 | W. G. Sebald (1944–2001), German novelist.

PAGE 245 | Bernard Simeone, *Cavatine* (Lagrasse: Verdier, 2000). Simeone (1957–2001), writer and a translator of Italian literature into French. See Jaccottet's *Ce peu de bruits* (Paris: Gallimard, 2008) for a tribute to Simeone (p. 15).

Stravinsky's 'Cantata' is a work for soprano, tenor, female choir and instrumental ensemble. It was composed in 1951–52.

PAGES 246–7 | Yves Bonnefoy, *Quarante-cinq poèmes de Yeats* (Paris: Hermann, 1989); *The Collected Poems of W. B. Yeats* (London: Macmillan, 1956), pp. 246–7.

PAGE 247 | Étienne Moulinié (1599–1676), baroque music composer.

Franz Kafka, *Journaux*, Volume 3 (Paris: Gallimard-Pléiade, 1984). In German, respectively:

'Viele Schatten der Abgeschiedenen beschäftigen sich
    nur damit, die Fluten des Totenflusses zu belecken,

weil er von uns herkommt und noch den salzigen
Geschmack unserer Meere hat.'

'Der Dornbusch ist der alte Weg-Versperrer. Er muß
Feuer fangen, wenn du weiter willst.'

'Ihnen entlaufen. Irgendein geschickter Sprung. Zu
Hause bei der Lampe im stillen Zimmer. Unvor-
sichtig, es zu sagen. Es ruft si aus den Wäldern,
wie wenn man die Lampe angezündet hätte, um
ihnen auf die Spur zu helfen.'

PAGE 251–2 | Maurice Scève (1501–c.1564), French poet and
author of *Délie, objet de plus haute vertu*. The first strophe
cited ('Great was the blow . . .') is translated in Michael
Giordano's *The Art of Meditation and the French Renais-
sance Love Lyric: The Poetics of Introspection in Maurice
Scève's 'Délie objet de plus haulte vertu'* (*1544*) (Toronto:
University of Toronto Press, 2010). The second strophe
('Thus I in your ungracious frost am lean . . .') is trans-
lated by Geoffrey Dutton, *Antipodes in Shoes* (Sydney:
Edwards & Shaw, 1958). The third poem ('White dawn
had barely finished crowning. . .') is translated by Richard
Sieburth, *Emblems of Desire: Selection from the Délie of
Maurice Scève* (New York: Archipelago Books, 2007). In
Ce peu de bruits, Jaccottet writes about the 12th-century
Japanese poet Saiygō Hōshi (1118–1190).

PAGE 253 | Jean-Christophe Bailly, *Le Champ mimétique*
(Paris: Seuil, 2005).

PAGES 253–4 | Cesare Pavese, *Disaffections: Complete Poems
1930–1950* (Geoffrey Brock trans., Port Townsend, WA:
Copper Canyon Press, 2002, p. 171).

PAGE 255 | For the translation of the remark by Plotinus
(*Enneads*, 2.3.7), see John Durham Peters' *The Marvelous*

Clouds: *Toward a Philosophy of Elemental Media* (Chicago: University of Chicago Press, 2015), p. 170.

PAGE 256 | Peter Handke, *Gestern unterwegs* (Berlin: Jung und Jung, 2005); *Hier en chemin* (translated into French by Olivier Le Lay, Lagrasse: Verdier, 2011).

Gustav Leonhardt (1928–2012) was a Dutch harpsichordist and conductor.

Bach's *English Suites* were probably composed in 1715.

PAGE 257 | Mallarmé's lines ('l'oiseau qu'on n'ouït jamais / une autre fois en la vie') are found in the second part of 'Petit air' (1914).

PAGE 258 | Jaccottet refers to Roud's *Campagnes perdues*: *Essai pour un paradis* (Saint Clément de Rivière: Fata Morgana, 1978).

Nicolas Poussin, *The Funeral of Phocion* (1648), a painting of which three versions are known, housed in the Louvre, the National Museum Cardiff and Glass House in New Canaan, Connecticut, respectively.